WHAT LEADERS ARE SAYING
ABOUT
SERVE YOUR CITY

Pastor Dino's new book, *Serve Your City*, is a message to the heart of every leader. He powerfully engages the church to not just "go" but take a look at "how we'll go" to engage more effectively in our communities, as we lovingly reach out to the disenfranchised, poor, overlooked and disadvantaged. The gospel means that we are all "sent ones." This book will open your eyes and give you a clear strategy. Pastor Dino activates the church to not just proclaim of the Good News of Jesus, but to *show* it tangibly to those in our spheres of life and influence.

ANDI ANDREW
Co-Pastor of Liberty Church, New York, New York
Author of *She Is Free; Learning the Truth About the Lies That Hold You Captive*

Dino Rizzo's book, *Serve Your City*, gives so much wisdom for church leaders on every level. This book is beneficial to everyone! For decades in his daily walk, Pastor Dino has demonstrated the principles of embodying the love of God as he tells people about gospel of grace. I am so thankful for this book!

MATTHEW BARNETT
Co-Founder of The Dream Center
Senior Pastor, Angelus Temple, Los Angeles, California

People won't line up to be judged, but they might line up to be loved. Judging people is a terrible evangelism method. Today, the world is hurting. Jesus loves the world, Jesus died for this world, and Jesus can heal hurting people in the world. Heaven is real. *Serve Your City* is a book about bringing Jesus to a hurting world. How can we earn the right to be heard? By showing the world we care.

ROBERT BARRIGER

Lead Pastor, Camino de Vida, Lima, Peru

Humble, bold, and generous. I have always been a big fan of my good friend, Dino Rizzo. He's one of those "what you see is what you get" kind of guys, with no pride or pretense anywhere around him. He's real, raw, broken, and redeemed. Also, he's one of the most hilarious men I know, which makes it even more powerful when he stabs you (with kindness) with the truth. This leadership guide, and the book it supports, *Servolution*, is a compelling and ridiculously practical game-changer that will transform your church and community if you put it into action.

RICK BEZET

Lead Pastor, New Life Church, Conway, Arkansas

Not many people naturally love deeply like Dino Rizzo, and few can start a *Servolution* and change the way churches love their communities. That's why this book is so necessary. While loving deeply may not be natural, it must not be negotiable. *Serve Your City* provides a blueprint to get what's on the inside of every believer out.

MICAHN CARTER

Lead Pastor, Together Church, Yakima, Washington

The heart of God is for the lost and the least, not one or the other. In *Serve Your City*, Pastor Dino connects the dots to show how churches can demonstrate compassion by providing tangible resources to hurting people. When the church reaches out to help the lost and the least, it gains more credibility and people's hearts are opened to receive the good news of Jesus. This is the model of ministry Jesus used. It's powerful, effective and it will change churches, cities, states, and the world!

HERBERT COOPER

Senior Pastor, People's Church, Oklahoma City, Oklahoma

Author of *But God Changes Everything*

I have had a front seat in Dino Rizzo's life for over 20 years. I know of no one who is more qualified to help hurting and marginalized people than him. His heart to help people in a tangible way exemplifies what it means to be the hands and feet of Christ. His new book, *Serve Your City*, is thoughtful, practical and even humorous about living the life God intends for all of us—a life that actually realizes its potential, a life that's open handed and open hearted, always ready to serve. Every business leader, pastor, missionary, student or anyone wanting to serve their city, state, and nation should read this book then simply take the next step. Your cities and communities will be forever changed.

LEE DOMINGUE

Founder of Kingdom Builders

Author of *Pearls of the King*

Associate Pastor at Church of the Highlands, Birmingham, Alabama

Those who have had the greatest impact in my life are not the ones who speak great sermons but who display God's love and power in their everyday life. The life-changing principles shared in this book will transform you, not because Dino speaks them, but because he has lived them! Dino continues to make a difference in the lives of everyone who steps into his path. If there was only one book you could choose to motivate you to live like Jesus, this would be the one! Dino, thank you for inspiring us all.

PASTOR MARC ESTES

Lead Pastor, City Bible Church, Portland, Oregon

President, Portland Bible College, President, CBC Global Family

This book is like gold to anyone who wants to live a life beyond the borders of self. It will draw you in, stir you up, and guide you to a bigger, better and more rewarding life.

KEVIN GERALD

Lead Pastor, Champions Centre, Tacoma, Washington

We have all heard the old adage, "Do as I say, not as I do." But in *Serve Your City*, my friend Dino Rizzo reminds us that if we are going to FINISH the Great Commission that Jesus called us to in Matthew 28, we must get outside the walls of the church and "go and make disciples . . ." For too long, the church has bottled up our blessings within the confines of the beautiful structures we have erected, but Jesus has commissioned us to be a church that announces and demonstrates His love in the streets, in the coffee shops, in the classroom, and in the local business. Thanks, Pastor Dino, for reminding us that the church needs to leave the building!

DR. TIM HILL

Church of God General Overseer, Cleveland, Tennessee

For over two decades, I've watched my friend Dino Rizzo model the love of Jesus by what he says as well as what he does. In *Serve Your City*, Dino inspires us all to balance our words and our deeds with the same inseparable alignment we see in the ministry of Christ. Both challenging and encouraging, this book reminds us that compassion isn't secondary to our mission—it's essential.

CHRIS HODGES

Senior Pastor, Church of the Highlands, Birmingham, Alabama

Author of *Fresh Air* and *The Daniel Dilemma*

Dino Rizzo is uniquely qualified to write this life-transforming book about impacting our communities for Christ. His heart of compassion has been demonstrated by the tangible mobilization of God's people to be a fruitful presence of Jesus in the cities of our nation and world. Our planet is desperate for a gospel that is portrayed through our faith, hope and love, lived out in both word and action. Dino describes how we can live missional lives that will open our eyes, break our hearts, and affect destiny by following the life that Jesus intended for all of us.

ROB HOSKINS

President, OneHope Inc., Pampano Beach, Florida

I absolutely love Dino Rizzo's heart for the Kingdom, for our communities, and for reaching people for Jesus. He is one of the great visionaries when it comes to church leadership in our day. Growing out of his own raw and real context of ministry, *Serve Your City* gives every reader a practical guide for understanding God's great love for lost and hurting people and how we can passionately strengthen our capacity to extend His love and hope to them. This book needs to be read because it is biblical and practical. The applied principles will lead churches to make an eternal difference in the lives of millions of unchurched people around the world.

DR. KENT INGLE

President, Southeastern University, Lakeland, Florida

The Bible says, "To whom much is given, much is required." I have known Pastor Dino Rizzo for over 30 years and have seen how he has led himself and others to live out this message on a daily basis. In *Serve Your City*, he shares practical steps from real experience for leading your team into a loving relationship with your community. As we live out this command from Jesus, we have a choice to either spend our lives on ourselves or with Jesus on others. Thank you, Dino, for writing a book that challenges us as leaders and gives us tools to meet that challenge.

ROB KETTERLING

Lead Pastor, River Valley Church, Apple Valley, Minnesota

Dino Rizzo wrote *Serve Your City* to encourage, challenge and show us how we can reach all people with the love of Christ, not just those that cross the threshold of our churches. His heart for people, and how he lives that out every day, make him someone I listen very closely to. Don't read this book unless you want to be encouraged and challenged in ways you have never been before.

PHIL KLEIN

Founder focus412 and Executive Coach

As an urban church planter, pioneering and pastoring in what's currently referred to as "the most unchurched city in America," I often find myself scratching my head and wondering, *How in the world do I unlock the heart of my city so I can reach more people for Jesus?* Like a key, this book will help you unlock the heart of your city, and it will also help you unlock the potential of your church. *Serve Your City* is the perfect reminder that great churches aren't simply built by good preaching or good programming, but by stooping down into the brokenness of humanity through serving, loving and caring for people as we share the life-changing message of Jesus.

JASON LAIRD

Lead Pastor, Sozo Church, San Francisco, California

Sometimes you meet people in this life, and you have to make an effort to love them. Dino is the opposite—he's easy to love and easy to follow. He carries so much joy and genuine compassion for people that even if he doesn't know you very well, you feel like family. In reality, anybody who claims to be a Christian *should* make people feel like that, but it's become a lost art. It's rare to find a man like Dino who exemplifies God's love to this extent. If I want my church to see what loving a city and loving individuals looks like, I can point them to Dino. In this book, he has given us some keys on how to mobilize love. Our cities need it, and this book is timely. Get it, and better yet, live it. That will be my goal!

CARL LENTZ
Senior Pastor, Hillsong Church, New York, New York
Author of *Own the Moment*

Dino understands the crucial difference between being a church IN the community and being a church FOR the community. This is a book about being FOR a community. Churches must become missionaries again. This book can help every pastor build that kind of church!

SHAWN LOVEJOY
CEO, CourageToLead.com
Author of *Be Mean About the Vision*

Serve Your City—I absolutely love the title, the message and the man who wrote this book. I believe the church needs this message more than any time in history, and I know no one more qualified to champion it than Dino Rizzo!

DAVID L. MEYER
CEO of Hand of Hope, Joyce Meyer Ministry

Dino Rizzo is the right man with the right mandate to proclaim and demonstrate the message of Christ to our world. We value the life and leadership of Dino to get the church beyond its walls to serve our communities. It's time to throw them the rope of hope in tangible ways. Thank God for Dino showing us and telling us how to take the gospel to the streets!

PHIL MUNSEY

Chairman, Champions Network of Churches

Under Joel Osteen and Lakewood Church, Houston, Texas

The fringe. Everyone knows what it's like to be the one out on the fringe; feeling unloved or unlovable, flawed, having made one too many mistakes, and yet, we've been brought close to The One who embraces outcasts like myself. Pastor Dino Rizzo is one who speaks with such heart and candor about reawakening the Church's role in not losing touch with those out on the fringe. Beware! This book will reawaken your own story and remind you of our original purpose in the Church which is to reach others.

DIANNA NEPSTAD

Co-Lead Pastor, Fellowship Church, Antioch, California

Pastor Dino Rizzo has again written a masterpiece on the heart of God. In *Serve Your City*, he encourages us to do more than just talk about the gospel, but to model it as we share it. He reminds us that Jesus cared for the physical needs of people as He preached and taught them. That's the model for our ministry, too. This book is a must-read for all church leaders.

BENNY PEREZ

Lead Pastor, Church LV, Las Vegas, Nevada

In this incredible book, Dino Rizzo doesn't just teach church leaders how to love and serve their communities. He *shows* them how to do it. He reminds us that the best way to grow a church is to love the lost. Churches that embrace the spiritual truths and practical tips in this book will be transformed in a powerful way. It is a must-read for today's church leaders!

MARK PETTUS

President, Highlands College, Birmingham, Alabama

Sincerity and authenticity are incredibly valuable leadership traits. The same people-loving, champion of the hurting, God-serving preacher of the gospel you've heard speak to thousands is the Dino Rizzo I know as a dear friend. Not only is he gregarious and beyond fun, he is also a brilliant thinker who knows how to strategically operationalize vision, especially vision that touches others through the work of mercy and justice. Dino has a special gift, and he shares it well. *Serve Your City* will inspire and equip you to effectively move beyond the shadows of your church buildings into the daily lives of the hurting with the love and compassion of Jesus.

DR. ROBERT RECORD

Director of Christ Health Center, Birmingham, Alabama

I truly believe that Dino Rizzo has been given a backstage pass into the heart of God. He has a clear message of how to demonstrate the gospel through living beyond yourself. *Serve Your City* will inspire you to go far beyond experiencing God's love for yourself, so you and your church become the tangible evidence of that love through serving people in need. I am a witness that the principles and strategies shared in the pages of this transformative book can revolutionize a city!

JIMMY ROLLINS

Lead Pastor of i5 Church, Odenton, Maryland

Dino Rizzo is one of my dearest friends and an incredible man. The second you connect with Dino in any context, it's clear that his passion is people, and it's contagious. *Serve Your City* is a compelling, challenging and inspiring guide to taking church beyond the four walls of a building and make an eternal impact in your community. Not only will this book refuel your passion for reaching people, it also gives practical principles and methods you can put into practice for an immediate impact.

JOHN SIEBELING

Lead Pastor, The Life Church, Cordova, Tennessee

Dino Rizzo has been a friend who has inspired me for the last twenty years. I've never met someone with more compassion for those who are hurting, and I've watched God use him in amazing ways to make a difference. In *Serve Your City,* not only will you be inspired to a greater love for the people in your community, but you'll also learn how to grow a culture of compassion to serve your community with that love.

GREG SURRATT

President, Association of Related Churches

Founding Pastor, Seacoast Church, Charleston, South Carolina

To lead is to serve, and there's no one I know who lives this out with more passion or conviction than Dino. His life is an example of one dedicated to service. This book is a must-read if you want to make a greater impact on your city for Jesus. *Serve Your City* will do more than just inspire you. It will challenge the way you think and see ministry, empower you to lead, and equip you with all the practical resources you need to build a church that dares to go out and reach the world.

KYLE TURNER

Lead Pastor, The Cause Church, Kansas City, Missouri

Pastor Dino is truly one of a kind. He's a man that models what it looks like to be generous to all people. He genuinely sees their God-given potential and is willing to invest all that he can to bring out the very best in them. This book is an example of Pastor Dino's large heart for people. I hope you will lean into the message of this book, focus on every word, take notes, and really learn from a man who has lived this message.

CHAD VEACH

Lead Pastor of Zoe Church, Los Angeles, California

Dino doesn't just talk about love or preach about the love of Jesus. He shows the love of Jesus in the generous way that he lives. Dino was so generous in helping us plant Celebration Church twenty years ago. His fingerprints and the principles of this book are all over our church. We wouldn't be who we are as a church without the example, encouragement and equipping of Pastor Dino. I am so excited to share this book with our staff and the leaders of our church as we take the love of Christ outside of the four walls of the church and show the compassion of Christ to our city, our state and the world.

KERRI WEEMS

Co-Lead Pastor, Celebration Church, Jacksonville, Florida

I love this book and I love Dino. We have been friends for over twenty years, and we have done life and ministry together for a long time. I have had the privilege of a front row seat to watch Dino live out the truths in this book on a personal level and as a pastor. There are few people on planet Earth as qualified as Dino to help leaders and churches learn how to display the love of Jesus in their communities. You'll be inspired like I have been, and like our church has been, to reach out to the poor, the disadvantaged, the disenfranchised and the despised in very practical ways, and you and your church will be better because of it.

STOVALL WEEMS

Lead Pastor, Celebration Church, Jacksonville, Florida

SERVE YOUR CITY

HOW TO DO IT AND WHY IT MATTERS

DINO RIZZO

FOREWORD BY TOMMY BARNETT

ISBN: 978-1-64296-000-6
Published by ARC, The Association of Related Churches
First printing 2018
Printed in the United States

100% OF THE PROFITS FROM THIS BOOK GO TOWARD PLANTING CHURCHES THROUGH THE ASSOCIATION OF RELATED CHURCHES.

TABLE
OF CONTENTS

FOREWORD

By Tommy Barnett

I met Pastor Dino more than 20 years ago, and from our first conversation, I knew God had His hand on this remarkable man. We had a number of opportunities to minister together. One of the first trips was to Bangalore, India, for a Joyce Meyer Crusade in the city. Dino and I taught the pastors how to follow up with the people from their communities who were coming to the evening outreaches. One night in that crowded and beautiful city, we stayed up until 2:00 in the morning eating French fries and talking about God's heart for those the world has passed by. He was hungry to hear how our church back in Phoenix was providing tangible resources for the least and the gospel of grace for the lost. We were in the first stages of creating a Dream Center, and Dino wanted to know all about it. He asked how a pastor could carry the heavy weight of loving people who are struggling with addiction, poverty, homelessness, and violence.

I treasure the memory of that conversation, but it was only one of many. We've laughed and cried together, and we've talked about our families. We've waded into passages of Scripture that shape our ministries, and we've discussed the details of strategy. From the day we met, my relationship with Dino has been a treasure to me.

Serve Your City is Dino's life story, and I can honestly say it's also mine. He and Delynn are incredibly generous with their time and all the resources God has put in their hands, and they keep their hands open to share with others. Dino has partnered with us to establish and extend the ministry of our Dream Center. We couldn't have accomplished as much without his support and involvement. For over a decade, he has sent teams from his church to serve at our Dream Center, but his influence isn't limited to Baton Rouge, Birmingham, Phoenix, or Los Angeles. He is a champion of compassion. He has significantly shaped the conversation for church planters and pastors of established churches to make outreach in their communities an integral part of their mission and strategy.

Today, we face unprecedented challenges in our culture: more people than ever before need our help. We need to put aside our petty prejudices and reach out to love people. We can't wait for people to come to our churches. We must go to them, to meet them where they are, with hearts full of love and open hands of generosity, all directed by the wisdom God's Spirit provides. The truths and strategies in this book give us hope that we can make a difference. We can go outside our walls to love people the way Jesus loved people in His day . . . by *showing* them compassion while *telling* them about God's great grace.

Don't miss Dino's heart, and don't miss the clear strategy in this book. The world is waiting for us to love them.

TOMMY BARNETT
SENIOR PASTOR OF DREAM CITY CHURCH
Phoenix, Arizona

THE WORLD
IS WAITING
FOR US TO
LOVE THEM.

— TOMMY BARNETT —

You are unique! Don't live in self-doubt. Realize that whatever you see as a flaw or a lack is an opportunity for God to use that beautiful place of vulnerability for His glory. We are all out of our element in some way. We are all in need of God's grace and His miracles.

MATTHEW BARNETT

Misfits Welcome

INTRODUCTION

INTRODUCTION

WHEN I WAS A BOY...

When I was a boy, I struggled with delayed speech, and I had difficulty pronouncing certain consonants. In the first grade, I was put in a special class called "resource." This was before there was much sensitivity to these kinds of problems, so every day after home room, I got up and went to the class that carried plenty of emotional and relational baggage. There, I received speech therapy for half of each school day. I couldn't pronounce certain sounds, and I stuttered badly. Over the years, my speech patterns didn't improve very much, so I stayed in this class until I was in the eighth grade. At lunchtime each day, I left resource and went to the regular classes for the afternoon. As you might imagine, I wasn't exactly an exemplary student, but in the regular classes, I excelled in two subjects: honors recess and show and tell. I killed it in both of those.

At the end of the fifth grade, our teacher scheduled a Show and Tell Grand Finale, a Super Bowl of show and tell. She told us to bring something from our homes to present and tell everyone about it. To keep things fairly under control, so nobody brought snakes or too many Barbie dolls, our teacher asked us to write down what we planned to bring. She didn't want any

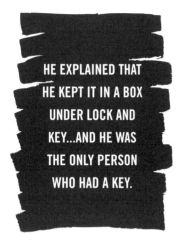

HE EXPLAINED THAT HE KEPT IT IN A BOX UNDER LOCK AND KEY...AND HE WAS THE ONLY PERSON WHO HAD A KEY.

duplications. By the time the paper got to me, almost everybody else had signed it. Only two of us were left—Johnny and me. After I'd written what I planned to bring, I handed the paper to Johnny. To my dismay, he wrote the same thing: a GI Joe Action Figure. I was so upset.

For the next couple of days, kids in our class brought their treasured items to class and told us all about them. I don't want to say these kids were competitive, but everybody was trying to one-up the others. Finally, Johnny had his turn. He smirked at me as he walked to the front of the class, and he proudly showed his GI Joe . . . in its original box! Oh, come on. What red-blooded boy still has the box his action figure came in? He described it as "a Special Edition GI Joe." He explained that he kept it in a box under lock and key . . . and he was the only person who had a key.

The teacher asked him, "Johnny, would you like to pass it around so everybody can see it up close?"

He exploded, "NO! I'm not letting anyone touch it! I keep it locked in my closet . . . with all my other collector GI Joes!"

Johnny sat down. The teacher turned to me and asked, "Dino, are you ready to show and tell?"

I nodded, "You bet I am!"

I guess I broke the rules because even though I knew Johnny was bringing his GI Joe, I brought mine anyway. I didn't care who else brought one—it was my pride and joy. When I walked to the front, I told the class, "This is my GI Joe, but it doesn't live in a box in the closet. It lives in the mud in my backyard . . . next to our dog that's on a chain!"

> I HADN'T KEPT MY GI JOE IN ITS ORIGINAL BOX LOCKED IN A CLOSET. IT HAD BEEN TO WAR...

I wasn't through. I pointed to a black place on its head and told them, "I lit his hair on fire." I then turned it over and showed them a gash on its back. "This is where I taped an M-80 to it and blew it up. And one of the legs came off, so I duct taped it back on. I've thrown it, run over it, and stomped on it, and it keeps coming back for more." I grabbed my GI Joe by the head and threw it. I yelled, "Catch, Johnny!"

I hadn't kept my GI Joe in its original box locked in a closet. It had been to war, and it had more than its share of bumps and bruises. The other kids in the class gave me a standing ovation.

This may seem like an odd story to introduce the subject of serving our communities, but actually, it fits perfectly. The Christian life isn't meant to be lived carefully protected in a box, and certainly not in a box on a shelf in a locked closet. It's meant to be lived in the real world, in the mud with real people, giving them real hope.

Far too often, people come to church, sing a little and hear a message, all within the walls of the church building, but their lives remain protected and secure, almost like they live in a box. We wonder why our people aren't more passionate, more committed to reach people with the gospel, and more willing to sacrifice to care for the disadvantaged. Don't get me wrong. I'm all for wonderful music and terrific teaching. That's important, but if we thumb through the pages of the Gospels, we see a very different model of leadership. Jesus' life and ministry are the ultimate example of show and tell. His followers saw Him heal the sick, feed the hungry, and care for the poor—and while He was doing those things, He taught them. That's His model: He showed them, and He told them. Sometimes, the model in our churches is limited to telling, with very little showing. I'm not criticizing or condemning. I'm just pointing to a different model, one that I stumbled on and found incredibly effective, one that I now see on every page of the accounts of the life of Jesus. I've learned that "show and tell" is the most powerful way to supercharge the hearts and release the energy of people in our churches. That's what this book is about.

"THE CHURCH CAME TO ME"

WHEN I WAS GROWING UP...

When I was growing up, I helped my parents in our family business in Myrtle Beach, South Carolina. We sold tourists lots of flip-flops, airbrushed shirts, shark teeth, and cotton candy, so we worked every weekend. It wasn't that we were against God or the church, but we were really busy every Saturday and Sunday. In fact, Sunday was our biggest day, and we couldn't afford to miss any potential customers. My dad was a "lapsed Catholic," but he was very generous, and my mom was a Baptist, but she didn't go to church regularly at all. Our family life revolved around selling candy apples, rabbits' feet, and mood rings. It was our livelihood, our reason for existence.

My older sister found Christ through a Billy Graham Crusade, but by my late teenage years, she was out of the house. There were a few passing moments when God surfaced in our lives, but going to church was literally the last thing on my mind.

By the time I was 17 years old, I had seen street preachers who yelled at people as they walked by, and I'd seen busloads of church people file onto the beach to pass out tracts that warned people they were going to some form of eternal condemnation. One day, a man came by our stand as I was putting out a display of shark teeth, and he struck up a conversation with me. He let me know pretty soon that he was a Christian, but he didn't yell, he didn't push, and he didn't pass out any literature that threatened me with gruesome, everlasting torment. He asked if I'd like a snowball from a vendor nearby. He wasn't in a hurry, and he didn't appear to have a pressing need to convert me. From the look in his eyes, the tone of his voice, and his genuine kindness, I felt something I hadn't felt from other Christians who had come to convert me: I felt seen . . . I felt noticed . . . and I felt loved.

I realized he actually had a specific agenda. Purely and simply, it was to love me. He didn't see me as a potential notch in his evangelism belt. He was genuinely interested in me, and he wanted to show God's love for me by listening to my story. After about half an hour of relaxed interaction, he asked if he could tell me how to know God. He explained the gospel in a simple message: accept, believe, confess. He asked, "Do you want me to pray with you to receive Christ?"

I said, "No, not really. Not right now."

I FELT SEEN...
I FELT NOTICED...
AND I FELT LOVED.

He wasn't offended, and he didn't threaten me. He smiled and said, "That's fine. Let me give you this piece of paper so in case you think of our conversation again, it will remind you what we talked about." He paused a second, and then he smiled again: "There may be a moment when you want to say 'yes' to the love of God. This piece of paper has all you need to know. When that moment comes, read the prayer on the back."

Two weeks later, I came home after being out late . . . at a place where I never should have gone. I had left the paper near my bed. At that moment, my heart felt drawn to Christ. I read the sheet again and decided to pray the prayer on the back. Immediately I sensed the love of God, the same love that man had displayed in our talk near the beach. He was a man I'd never met before, sent by a church I'd never visited (or heard of), trained by leaders who understood the power of kindness, and resourced by faithful people who tithed to God's kingdom. From the moment we met, I could tell I wasn't just a project to him. He genuinely loved me with the wonderful love of God.

I would never have gone to that church or any other one, but through him, the church came to me. I didn't take the initiative to reach out. This man and the people of this church didn't wait for me. He looked for a lost sheep, and he found one.

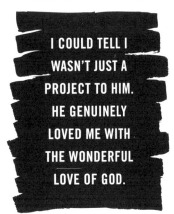

Today, many churches are incredibly attractive places. They have coffee bars, outstanding childcare, theatre seating, fantastic music, movie nights, family activities, and every other conceivable convenience. I'm not knocking those perks. As a matter of fact, I love all those features, and I'm a part of great churches that offer amazing things to people who arrive at their doors. I'm only observing there are plenty of people who will never make the first move to go to church to experience all the great things they have to offer. A lot of people are just like me: they need the church to come to them before they're willing to go to church.

> **"**
>
> **A LOT OF PEOPLE ARE JUST LIKE ME: THEY NEED THE CHURCH TO COME TO THEM.**
>
> **"**

The question isn't "Will we go to them?" If we understand the gospel and look at the life of Jesus, of course we'll go. The real question is how we'll go to them. In this book (and in everything I do), I want to help church leaders engage more effectively with people in their communities—especially those people who aren't going to take the first step toward the church.

TWO ASSUMPTIONS

I KNOW TWO IMPORTANT THINGS

I know two important things about pastors and other church leaders: First, they genuinely care about the people in their communities, and second, they're already incredibly busy. If they perceive the calling to reach out to the lost and the least as "one more thing on the to-do list," it won't happen. Already, far too many people and issues are demanding their time and attention. They need to rethink, redefine, and relocate their sense of calling. Reaching out to the poor, the disadvantaged, the disenfranchised, and the despised is central to the heart of God. It's not an addendum to the gospel of grace; it is the gospel of grace because all of us were alienated from God and needed Jesus to reach out to us with His sacrificial love.

As leaders, we may have many different motivations for being in the ministry, but they all revolve around reaching people with the love of Jesus Christ to impact their eternity. We have different gifts and we serve in different situations, but this is our common calling.

Jesus didn't wait for us to come to Him. He left the comfort and glory of heaven to come into our neighborhood. The incarnation is the greatest act of community engagement in the history of the world! He came as the King, but not like any king the planet had ever known. He was born in obscurity, and His parents were so poor they could afford only doves for an offering when He was presented at the temple. In His ministry, He moved effortlessly between the powerful and the powerless. But in fact, He demonstrated God's preference for the poor as He reached out to the

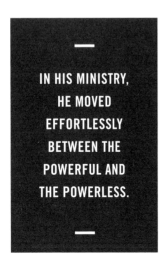

IN HIS MINISTRY, HE MOVED EFFORTLESSLY BETWEEN THE POWERFUL AND THE POWERLESS.

sick, lepers, the lame, those who were demon-possessed, foreigners, children, women, and others who were overlooked or despised by society. These people weren't projects to Jesus. He genuinely loved them, and they knew it.

To me, one of the most powerful and touching moments in the Gospels is John's short introduction to the scene when Jesus gathered the disciples for the Last Supper. John tells us, "It was just before the Passover Feast. Jesus knew that the time had come for him to leave this world and go to the Father. Having loved his own who were in the world, he now showed them the full extent of his love" (John 13:1). Jesus didn't show His love through a lecture; He showed it by taking the role of a servant, the lowest servant, and washing their dusty feet. The disciples (like us) were slow to get the point. They were soon bickering about which of them would occupy the highest positions when Jesus was crowned king. Things didn't turn out exactly like they planned!

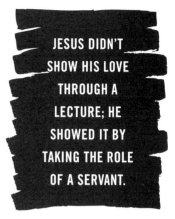

JESUS DIDN'T SHOW HIS LOVE THROUGH A LECTURE; HE SHOWED IT BY TAKING THE ROLE OF A SERVANT.

The next day, Jesus went to the ultimate lengths to show His love: He gave himself in our place on the cross. Jesus served the lost, the poor, the disenfranchised, and the forgotten. He didn't just tell us about "the full extent of his love"; He demonstrated it. From the beginning of the church, caring for the lost and the least has been central to our calling. To lead is to serve, and in fact, to believe is to serve.

For pastors and other church leaders, an act of compassion for those who feel overlooked isn't just one more priority to add to our to-do list. Caring for "the least of these" is the culture of the gospel, something we can't afford to miss if we're to be who God wants us to be. But we need to be observant. The strategies we use should be tailored to the needs we uncover wherever we live—in rural areas, small towns, suburbs, and cities. We need to move our focus outside the walls of our buildings. The church isn't a place, and it isn't restricted to a time on Sunday or any other time of the week. We are people who have been chosen, forgiven, loved, and adopted by God. We belong to Him all day every day, and we have the unspeakable privilege of being channels of His grace, wisdom, and strength to people who never expected to receive God's amazing love. We're on a rescue mission to reach people who are stranded. Some know how desperate their situations are, but some are completely unaware. Like Jesus, we wade into their lives with tangible help—food, shelter, clothing, and safety—and the incomparable message of grace. As they see love in action and hear the good news, we let them choose to accept His gracious offer.

The benefits of making this ministry central to the calling of your church are deep and wide. You and your people will be more in touch with the heart of God, you'll see specific results in the lives of those in need, your people will grow in their love for God and for people as they see God use them, and people in your community will be drawn to the love and joy they've experienced. In other words, your church will grow as people in your community feel loved. Those results are worth the effort.

How does all this happen? We need to hold two truths in our hands: First, God is already using your people to care for the people around them. The gospel has changed them from selfish to generous, and they're responding to the needs they see every day. You don't have to drum up their enthusiasm. Your job is to celebrate their compassion, provide resources, and empower them to lead. Second, you need the Spirit's power working through a God-inspired plan to create a culture of generosity in your church. When the church began, virtually all believers were Jews; Gentiles were considered outsiders, unclean and despicable. God used a vision and a visitor to prompt Peter to travel to the home of Cornelius, a Roman soldier, to share the gospel of grace. Peter explained how remarkable it was that God was now inviting Gentiles to be His children.

WE'RE ON A RESCUE MISSION TO REACH PEOPLE WHO ARE STRANDED.

He began by telling Cornelius about the life and purpose of Jesus: "You know the message God sent to the people of Israel, announcing the good news of peace through Jesus Christ, who is Lord of all. You know what has happened throughout the province of Judea, beginning in Galilee after the baptism that John preached—how God anointed Jesus of Nazareth with the Holy Spirit and power, and how he went around doing good and healing all who were under the power of the devil, because God was with him" (Acts 10:36–38).

But Peter wasn't finished with his explanation. Yes, Jesus came first to the Jews, but His love extends to all people. In fact, the wide scope of God's grace shouldn't have been a surprise to anyone. Peter continued, "He commanded us to preach to the people and to testify that he is the one whom God appointed as judge of the living and the dead. All the prophets testify about him that everyone who believes in him receives forgiveness of sins through his name" (Acts 10:42–43).

The church began with a heart for diversity. Then and now, no one is beyond the grace of God, and no one is beyond the reach of God's people. Some of our acts of compassion are stirred spontaneously as the love we experience flows through us and from us into the lives of others, but churches need a plan. Through Isaiah, God connected the dots: "But a generous man devises generous things, and by generosity he shall stand" (Isaiah 32:8, NKJV). Pastors and church leaders, it's our job to "devise generous things" our people can be involved in.

LET ME ASK A FEW QUESTIONS:

— AS WE LOOK AT THE PRIORITIES JESUS DEMONSTRATED, HOW WELL DO OURS MATCH HIS?

— IS OUR CHURCH KNOWN IN THE COMMUNITY FOR ITS COMPASSION TOWARD DISADVANTAGED PEOPLE?

— HOW WOULD WE EXPLAIN THE HEART OF GOD FOR OUR COMMUNITIES?

— HOW MANY OF OUR RESOURCES ARE WE ALLOCATING TO CARE FOR THE POOR AND THE DISADVANTAGED?

— ARE THE RESOURCES AND TIME WE INVEST IN PEOPLE HELPING THEM TAKE THE NEXT STEP OUT OF THEIR CIRCUMSTANCES AND INTO A PLACE WHERE THEY CAN CONNECT WITH THE BODY OF CHRIST?

You already care for people outside the walls of your church, or you wouldn't have picked up this book. I simply want to share some stories and lessons I've learned as we've taken the initiative to reach out to the people in our community. We've done some pretty cool things, but we've made plenty of mistakes. I want to help you avoid some of our mistakes. (Don't worry, you'll make enough of your own!) I'll give you a glimpse of where we've found some valuable resources that have enabled us to care for more people. And finally, I want to encourage you to stay on task through the inevitable ups and downs as you reach out to hurting, displaced, overlooked people.

HELPFUL TOOLS

HELPFUL TOOLS

This book is one of several tools we are providing for you and your people:

We're recommending my book, *Servolution*, for every person in your church to be inspired to joyfully and effectively serve others.

The book you hold in your hands is for pastors and leaders—probably the staff team, key volunteers, and small group leaders. A serving culture starts with leadership. This book is designed to help leaders understand the heart of serving and provide a strategy for community outreach.

In addition, we are also providing an extensive and expanding array of online resources that can help you with planning and implementation (e.g., small group curriculum, podcasts, and webinars).

For more information about resources, go to the Appendix, Additional Resources.

AS YOU READ *SERVE YOUR CITY* AND GO THROUGH IT WITH OTHER LEADERS, YOU CAN RESHAPE YOUR PRIORITIES TO MAKE SURE YOU'RE IN LINE WITH GOD'S HEART AND HIS PURPOSES.

MY HOPE FOR YOU

As you READ THIS BOOK

As you read this book and take steps to reach out more effectively to your community, I hope the stories inspire you and the ideas propel your planning. You can do this. You can have an effective presence in your community. You can see God use your people to transform lives and bring hope to the hopeless. You'll learn to go with full hearts and open hands. The people you serve may never darken the door of your church, but that's just fine. Only one of the lepers Jesus healed turned around to thank Him, but He kept reaching out, offering himself, healing bodies, and changing lives.

Actually, this ministry is easier than you can imagine. In fact, it's already happening as your people care for their neighbors and strangers. Your task isn't to make people care; it's only to develop the people God has given you so they will in turn develop others. You'll provide "gospel logistics" for the "points of compassion" that already exist in your people, and you'll inspire small groups and teams to find creative, effective ways to make a difference in the community. You'll give your people focus, supplies, encouragement, and connections to even more people. As this ministry unfolds, you'll uncover more gifts, talents, and resources than you ever imagined.

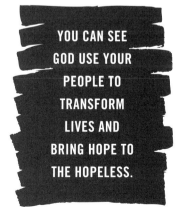

YOU CAN SEE GOD USE YOUR PEOPLE TO TRANSFORM LIVES AND BRING HOPE TO THE HOPELESS.

People who have very practical skills—carpentry, sewing, money management, auto repair, computer repair, etc., etc.—will come out of the woodwork to use them to help people.

Those who attend your church already love God and the people around them, but you can help them have a far greater impact . . . on the people next door to them and the people they would have never met without the church's community involvement. As we dive deeper into the love of God, His love flows out in bigger, deeper, wider, and more specific ways. Our task—and our privilege—is to point our people to the grace Jesus pours out on us who are so undeserving so that our hearts melt with love for others who have royally messed up their lives. When we're in touch with the heart of God, we see poor people differently, we see addicts and alcoholics through changed eyes, our hearts break for those who are heartbroken, and we want them to experience the wonder of God's kindness and compassion.

OUR LIVES MOVE AT THE SPEED OF THE PAIN WE PERCEIVE IN THOSE AROUND US.

Our lives move at the speed of the pain we perceive in those around us. If we're unaware or uncaring, we fly past them, but if we notice and care, we slow down to provide love and resources for them. On a larger scale, I believe the church moves at the speed of the pain we perceive in our communities. Jesus was never in a hurry. He stopped to listen, to touch, to care, and His love changed people. It still does. The pain of people outside the church is hard to notice if our attention is fixed on what happens inside the church. One of our main tasks as leaders, then, is to give people permission to take God's love and power outside the building.

What kind of difference do you want to make? What legacy are you crafting and leaving behind? If it's only excellence and size, you're missing the heart of God. But if you have the unmitigated thrill of seeing your people step into the lives of the lost and the least in your community, you'll leave a powerful legacy of compassion and strength to your leaders, your people, and everyone they touch. Jesus used "show and tell" to move people to action, and we can use the same communication strategy. Telling our people to be compassionate isn't enough. Like Jesus with His disciples, we need to take our people with us to touch the lives of those who are often overlooked. When we do this, amazing things happen. I know. I've seen it.

Don't miss the power of show and tell. It matters.

The principles and applications in this book were shaped by many years of trial and error as I've tried to take the love, power, and grace of God to people who often feel forgotten. But these ideas aren't unique to me. ARC churches are doing amazing, creative, and powerful outreaches. In these chapters, you'll find stories from other ARC churches mobilizing their people to take the love of God to people in their communities.

At the end of this introduction and each chapter, you'll find some questions. I encourage you to use these as you consider the what, why, and how of your church's strategy to serve your community. You can also use the questions to promote discussions among your leadership team. You'll get a lot more out of this book if you take time to think, pray, and talk about the stories and principles.

ISAIAH 58:6-9

"Is not this the kind of fasting I have chosen:
to loose the chains of injustice
   and untie the cords of the yoke,
to set the oppressed free
   and break every yoke?
Is it not to share your food with the hungry
   and to provide the poor wanderer with shelter—
when you see the naked, to clothe them,
   and not to turn away from your own flesh and blood?
Then your light will break forth like the dawn,
   and your healing will quickly appear;
then your righteousness will go before you,
   and the glory of the LORD will be your rear guard.
Then you will call, and the LORD will answer;
   you will cry for help, and he will say: Here am I."

THINK ABOUT IT

1

What are some reasons it's easy for church leaders to invest a disproportionate amount of time, energy, and money on what happens within the walls of the church instead of what happens beyond them?

....

....

....

....

....

....

2

A lot of people never show up at church because they have a negative perception of what goes on in the building. What are some ways we can give people a positive perception of Jesus and the church before they walk through our doors?

....

....

....

....

....

....

3

Who are some people
in your church who
are already involved in
compassionate care for
others? What impact are
they having?

....

....

....

....

....

....

....

....

....

....

4

What do you hope to
get out of this book —
for you and for your
leadership team?

....

....

....

....

....

....

....

....

....

....

5

If you're leading a discussion with your team, write the answers to these questions on a whiteboard:

Why was our church started in the first place?

What are your dreams to reach our city?

When you think of making a difference in the town or city, what faces come to mind?

Who are some people in your church who see the church's mission as a powerful blend of compassion for the poor and the gospel for all?

....
....
....
....
....
....
....
....
....
....
....
....
....
....
....
....
....
....
....
....
....

The "least of my brethren" are the hungry and the lonely, not only for food, but for the Word of God; the thirsty and the ignorant not only for water, but also for knowledge, peace, truth, justice and love; the naked and the unloved, not only for clothes but also for human dignity; the unwanted; the unborn child; the racially discriminated against; the homeless and abandoned, not only for a shelter made of bricks, but for a heart that understands, that covers, that loves; the sick, the dying destitutes, and the captives, not only in body, but also in mind and spirit; all those who have lost all hope and faith in life; the alcoholics and dying addicts and all those who have lost God (for them God was but God is) and who have lost all hope in the power of the Spirit.

MOTHER TERESA
A Simple Path

CHAPTER ONE

CONNECTING WITH GOD'S HEART

WHEN I HAD BEEN

When I had been a Christian only about two weeks, I walked to my car late one night after work and noticed a woman digging around in a trashcan behind a fast-food restaurant. The alley was dark, but there was enough light for me to see her clearly. I'm sure I'd seen poor, homeless people looking through trash before, but this was the first time I really noticed. The gospel was changing my heart and giving me new eyes to see the people around me. As I watched her, I thought, *It shouldn't be this way!*

The next day, she came by the counter of our tourist shop at Myrtle Beach. There was no question it was the same lady, but I don't think she recognized me from the night before. My heart broke for her, but I wasn't sure what to do. I knew she was hungry, so I stammered, "Would you wait here for a minute?" She looked a little confused, but she nodded.

I went to the nearest McDonald's and bought 40 one-dollar certificates. I almost ran back to the counter. I wasn't sure she'd still be there, but she was waiting patiently. When I gave the certificates to her, she looked startled. For the first time in my life, I said the words, "I just want you to know that

Jesus loves you." I didn't give her a theological discourse on the meaning of the incarnation and the cross. That one line was all I had. The sentence that came out of my mouth was the sum total of all the theology I knew, the entirety of all I had to tell.

I didn't give her the certificates and tell her Jesus loves her because I had been trained to do those things. I wasn't doing it for any reward or to be noticed. It was merely an expression of the love God had shown me, and I wanted her to experience His love, too. The grace of God had taken my breath away, and I wanted to share the wonder of His grace with that dear woman.

She came by our counter a number of times that summer, often just to talk. I'm sure she was lonely, and she was glad to have someone—anyone!—connect with her. We had absolutely nothing in common, but this fact didn't matter to either of us. I bought her a few more meals, but mostly, we became friends and just talked. By the middle of the summer, I began attending a church, and a woman in the church reached out to her to become another friend.

THERE'S A DIFFERENCE BETWEEN SEEING A NEED AND MEETING IT.

Our encounter with Jesus changes our hearts and gives us empathy for others who are broken and needy. There's a difference, though, between seeing a need and meeting it, between intention and action. It's not enough to notice. Jesus noticed our need, and He moved heaven and earth to meet it. Loving, sacrificial action is the measure of His love, and it's the measure of our love, too.

We have an array of excuses to notice but not help. I know because I've used them. But something wonderful happens when the love of God overcomes our resistance. Not long ago I passed a man who was standing next to his car on the side of the road. Instantly, I thought, *Man, I'm really busy, and I have no idea how long it would take to help him.* And I also thought, *I am absolutely the last person anyone would ask for help with anything mechanical!* But I sensed the Holy Spirit ask me a simple question: "Will you stop to help him?"

SOMETHING WONDERFUL HAPPENS WHEN THE LOVE OF GOD OVERCOMES OUR RESISTANCE.

I turned around and drove back. When I stopped behind him and got out of my truck, I asked, "Hey, man, are you good? Do you need anything?" (Probably not the most brilliant questions anyone could ask someone stranded on the side of the road!)

He told me, "My car's running hot. I need some water for the radiator."

I happened to have some bottles of water in my truck. Instantly, I realized God had made me adequate for this moment. After he poured the water in his radiator, he thanked me for stopping. I said, "Hey, I want you to know that God had me stop to help you. I couldn't have helped you with anything if your car needed a mechanic, but I had the water you needed. You know God's got you, don't you? He must love you a lot for Him to tell me to turn around and come back to help you!" We both laughed, he gave me a high five, and we drove off.

The questions for me, and my guess is that the questions for you and everyone in your church, are: Are we listening to the voice of the Spirit? And will we obey when the Holy Spirit directs us to step into someone's life to care? The issue isn't our talent, our resources, or our abilities. The issue is whether we are in tune with the heart of God for people in need.

We often focus on Jesus' actions, but if we look more closely at the Gospels, we'll notice that Jesus' attention was often captured by those in need. Time and time again, when He heard people cry out or He noticed them in need, He stopped to listen, to care, to touch, and to heal.

NOT AN ADD-ON

WHEN WE READ THE SCRIPTURES,

When we read the Scriptures, we repeatedly see God's heart for the vulnerable people in society. From the earliest pages of the Bible, God instructed His people to care for widows, orphans, the poor, and immigrants. (Today we would add single moms, addicts, the elderly, the homeless, women who have been trafficked, and other vulnerable groups.) This care wasn't designed to rob people of their self-respect, but to build and nurture it. For example, farmers were to leave the edges around their fields so poor people could harvest enough grain for their bread. Through Isaiah, God condemned His people for doing all the "right things" in worship and fasting but neglecting to care for the poor among them. God even blasted the pagan kingdoms and held them accountable for refusing to care for the disadvantaged.[1]

---

1   For much more on the teaching of Scripture in the Old and New Testaments about God's heart for the poor, see *Generous Justice* by Timothy Keller.

When Jesus began His ministry by reading from the scroll of Isaiah, He connected His mission with God's heart described in the ancient Scriptures:

> He stood up to read, and the scroll of the prophet Isaiah was handed to him. Unrolling it, he found the place where it is written:
>
> "The Spirit of the Lord is on me,
>   because he has anointed me
>   to proclaim good news to the poor.
> He has sent me to proclaim freedom for the prisoners
>   and recovery of sight for the blind,
> to set the oppressed free,
>   to proclaim the year of the Lord's favor." (Luke 4:16–19)

Jesus was prejudiced, but not in the way we usually use this word. He was prejudiced *toward people who needed help.* He loved everybody, rich and poor, powerful and powerless, but the Gospel writers made sure we understand that Jesus took special pains to reach out to those who were despised, overlooked, and rejected. His personal space and His comfort were secondary. He delighted to demonstrate His love and power in the lives of those who were on the fringes of society.

The world hasn't changed much since the first century. The powerful, the rich, and the beautiful expect to rule. Christians, however, have a very different value system. We are connected to the One who gave away power, who became last so He could put us first, whose only clothes were

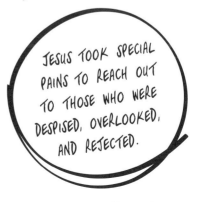

JESUS TOOK SPECIAL PAINS TO REACH OUT TO THOSE WHO WERE DESPISED, OVERLOOKED, AND REJECTED.

gambled for, who died without a dime in His pocket, and in fact, was buried in a borrowed tomb. His heart was (and is) diametrically opposite of the values of our world.

We have an incredible number of opportunities to step into the lives of hurting people. When the worst happens, Christians are the best thing to happen to a town or a city. When someone is gravely sick or killed, those who have experienced the compassion of Jesus weep with those who weep. When natural disasters destroy a community, those whose hearts are filled with faith, hope, and love step in to provide a shoulder to cry on, some sweat and labor to fix things, and to fill a hungry stomach or two. When times are difficult and dark, Christians shine like lights in a troubled world. In a world with so much hate and division, we show and tell people about the healing love of Jesus.

Throngs of people were drawn to Jesus because He was so different from anything they had seen in their stiff, demanding, legalistic religious leaders. In His most famous sermon, Jesus taught them about the love of God, the grace of God, and the purposes of God, and "the crowds were amazed at his teaching" (Matthew 7:28). The story, though, wasn't finished. When Jesus came down from the mountain, He healed a man with leprosy (Matthew 8:1–4), a centurion's servant who was paralyzed (Matthew 8:5–13), and Peter's mother-in-law (Matthew 8:14–15), and He drove demons out of those who were possessed (Matthew 8:16–17).

My favorite scene is also recorded by Matthew:

> Jesus left there and went along the Sea of Galilee. Then he went up on a mountainside and sat down. Great crowds came to him, bringing the lame,

the blind, the crippled, the mute and many others, and laid them at his feet; and he healed them. The people were amazed when they saw the mute speaking, the crippled made well, the lame walking and the blind seeing. And they praised the God of Israel. (Matthew 15:29–31)

Jesus was consumed with the needs of others. He was with them, among them, touching them. Matthew tells us:

Jesus called his disciples to him and said, "I have compassion for these people; they have already been with me three days and have nothing to eat. I do not want to send them away hungry, or they may collapse on the way." (Matthew 15:32)

Jesus used a deli lunch of a few little loaves of bread and some sardines, and in another miraculous display, He fed all of them—four thousand men, plus their spouses and kids, maybe twelve thousand in all.

I get the idea this wasn't really an unusual day for Jesus! Wherever Jesus contacted people, He taught them, He loved them, He healed them, and He helped them. He never turned anyone away, but He was never in a hurry. He went to them; He didn't wait for them to come to Him. He was outside when He taught the crowd, but in intimate encounters, He touched and healed. At one point, four men dug a hole in the ceiling to drop their paralyzed friend in front of Jesus because the house

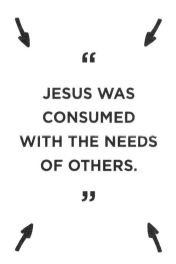

"

JESUS WAS CONSUMED WITH THE NEEDS OF OTHERS.

"

was too crowded for them to bring him in. And now, Jesus had ceiling tile falling on His head and a man coming through the hole! He was more than willing to have His personal space violated so He could show His love to people around Him.

TRANSFORMED BY LOVE

WHEN I WALK INTO A ROOM

When I walk into a room where there are a lot of people I don't know, I'm very self-conscious. I try to read people's expressions to see if they like me and accept me, and I want to impress them. (I'm sure I'm the only one like this, so pray for me!) Jesus doesn't seem to ever be self-conscious. In the most threatening circumstances, He was fully secure, aware of what was going on, and capable of responding with the full measure of truth and grace. And those who are filled with His love, forgiveness, and acceptance are becoming like Him: secure, no longer self-absorbed, and now aware of the needs of others.

> THOSE WHO ARE FILLED WITH HIS LOVE, FORGIVENESS, AND ACCEPTANCE ARE BECOMING LIKE HIM.

One of my favorite scenes in the Gospels is Luke's account of the dinner party at the home of Simon the Pharisee. In the middle of dinner, a woman burst in. She not only wasn't invited, Simon didn't want her there at all! She was probably a prostitute, and she must have met Jesus in a chance encounter on the street earlier that day. We don't know the specifics of their conversation, but one thing is clear: she experienced the wonder of His love and forgiveness. That night, she couldn't contain

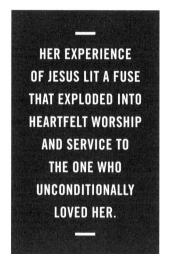

HER EXPERIENCE OF JESUS LIT A FUSE THAT EXPLODED INTO HEARTFELT WORSHIP AND SERVICE TO THE ONE WHO UNCONDITIONALLY LOVED HER.

herself. She found out where Jesus was having dinner. In spite of the fact this Pharisee despised "sinners" like her, she blew past the servants and threw herself at Jesus' feet. Luke tells us "she came there with an alabaster jar of perfume. As she stood behind him at his feet weeping, she began to wet his feet with her tears. Then she wiped them with her hair, kissed them and poured perfume on them" (Luke 7:37–38).

Simon was outraged that the woman had come uninvited, but Jesus took that glorious moment to draw a clear contrast: Simon, the self-righteous religious leader, had no love in his heart for the woman, and for that matter, for Jesus. But the woman, who had a life-changing encounter with Jesus only hours before, couldn't stop displaying her affection for Him. Her experience of Jesus lit a fuse that exploded into heartfelt worship and service to the One who unconditionally loved her. Who can doubt she left Simon's house and told everybody she knew about Jesus?

So...who are you and I in this story?

Are we like Simon, finding fault with Jesus, His methods and message, and in arrogance refusing to fully embrace Jesus' loving presence? No, probably not, but some people in our churches are like Simon. Some of us, though, are like the disciples, who by this time may have taken Jesus for granted. We may have been thrilled at one point, but now ministry is more of a grind. Or like the woman, is the incredible love of Jesus so rich and real to us that it keeps lighting the fuse of praise, gratitude, and glad service?

Here's another way to analyze and apply the lessons from this scene: What can we not stop doing? Is our default mode to criticize those who are different from us, to stand aloof from them, to find fault with their characters? Or have we been transformed like this woman so that our hearts burst with delight, love, and joy? Are we so insecure that we're "reading the room" instead of being fully present and attentive to people? Are we more concerned with our reputations or the hearts of the people we meet?

When you walk into a new situation (or any situation), soak up the love of Jesus so you don't need anyone's approval and you're not afraid of anyone's scowl. Dive deep into the grace of God and own the room like Jesus did when the woman came into Simon's house. Take the initiative to walk across the room to meet people (especially people who don't look like you), enter their world without a preconceived agenda, ask great questions, and listen like you really care . . . because you really do!

A pastor once told me he didn't like to engage others because he's an introvert. I told him being an introvert isn't a character flaw, but loving people isn't only the job description of extroverts. It's the calling, privilege, and command for every believer. We just do it in different ways.

Sometimes we have an idea that Jesus is the "stained glass" guy who is immobile and holding a lamb on His shoulders, or that He floats a few inches off the ground and is unapproachable. That's ridiculous. When we read the Gospels, we see Jesus mixing it up with every kind of person. Mark even starts his account with Jesus touching a leper! If

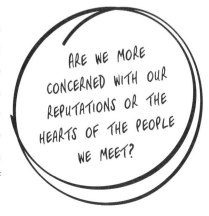

ARE WE MORE CONCERNED WITH OUR REPUTATIONS OR THE HEARTS OF THE PEOPLE WE MEET?

that doesn't get your attention, what will? Others may have avoided the outcasts of society, but not Jesus. He moved into the lives of the blind, the lame, children, women, foreigners, the poor, the sick, and those who were tormented by demons. He didn't avoid difficult people; He treasured them.

Jesus doesn't ask us to care out of empty hearts. If we see needy people as threats to our comfort, as irritations or annoyances, we need to experience the grace of God more deeply.

Graced people grace people.

Healed people heal people.

Forgiven people forgive people.

Loved people love people.

Accepted people accept people.

We don't wait until we have it all together before we step into the lives of others. We just need to be amazed at what God has done for us and is doing in us. That's enough, and that's plenty.

"

WE DON'T WAIT UNTIL WE HAVE IT ALL TOGETHER BEFORE WE STEP INTO THE LIVES OF OTHERS.

"

GRACED PEOPLE
GRACE PEOPLE.
HEALED PEOPLE
HEAL PEOPLE.
FORGIVEN PEOPLE
FORGIVE PEOPLE.
LOVED PEOPLE
LOVE PEOPLE.
ACCEPTED PEOPLE
ACCEPT PEOPLE.

Creating and developing a ministry to serve the community is much more than a program. It's a calling and an overflow of the love of God. If we connect to the heart of God, we'll inevitably reach into the recesses of our communities and uncover needs, hopes, and hurts that may have been in the dark for many years. Our experience of the matchless love of God enables us to move past our fears and out of our comfort zones so we become the hands, feet, and voice of Jesus.

SHIFTING THE CULTURE

A CULTURE OF COMPASSION

A culture of compassion begins with a conviction of brokenness. I can't be the leader God has called me to be unless I'm amazed that the Creator of the universe stooped low enough to come into our neighborhood to love, serve, and give himself to the point of death. Jesus cared to the ultimate lengths for "the least of these"—people like me. If I have the slightest inkling of His sacrificial love for me and for the whole world, I'll be passionate about caring for the people He cares for . . . which is every person on the planet.

I don't know many (actually, I don't know any) pastors who don't care deeply about the lost and the least in their communities. They care or they wouldn't have become pastors! But I also don't know many who aren't already drowning under a million things to do. They're busy, they're stressed, and they're not looking for another priority to add to their to-do list. In ministry, there is always tension between administration and pastoring people, between making things run efficiently and intentionally wading into the mess of people's lives. As one pastor put it, the gospel isn't just the minimum requirements for people to go to heaven when they die. The gospel is the power of God to transform us from the inside out, changing our values, our goals, our motives, and our relationships. We realize we are all equally lost, hopeless, and helpless without Christ, and we are all equally loved, forgiven, and accepted in Him. Grace shatters and humbles our sense of superiority, and it gives magnificent dignity to those who have felt inferior.

Every church (and every other group of people) has an identifiable culture that consists of the language, values, priorities, ways we relate to each other, what we celebrate and what makes us grieve. The existence of a culture doesn't mean it's necessarily a good one. Plenty of organizations have toxic or demeaning cultures. Leaders shape culture, so our task is to pour God's grace and compassion into the lives of our people so outreach in the community becomes second nature.

New church plants and small churches have an advantage in creating their culture because they don't have a huge ship to turn (and they don't have a lot of people who are resistant to change.) In these churches, the pastor has the opportunity to set the culture of caring from the beginning, even before the doors open for the first time. Established churches have a harder pull. When a culture is already established and has become ingrown, a fresh injection of enthusiasm and activism almost always meets a mixed response: some are excited and some think you've gone nuts! Turning the ship is certainly possible, but it requires a blend of diplomacy and tenacity. Dying churches have lost their heart for outreach. They need

"

GRACE SHATTERS AND HUMBLES OUR SENSE OF SUPERIORITY.

"

a resurrection, a complete re-fabrication of their values, priorities, and activities.

Change always involves hard choices. In established churches, pastors who want to change the culture need to decide who they're going to make uncomfortable—because it's inevitable that some will be. Quite often, the young (those who don't give much) are excited about caring for the disadvantaged, and older people (whose tithes are the foundation of the budget) are the most resistant. Courageous pastors will lose some people and attract some others. Change, then, is a colossal threat as well as a wonderful opportunity.

OUR TASK IS TO POUR GOD'S GRACE AND COMPASSION INTO THE LIVES OF OUR PEOPLE.

If you're trusting God to use you to transform an ingrown culture to an outreach culture, be prepared for plenty of fears to surface and false assumptions to be expressed. When you talk about caring for the poor, homeless, addicts, and immigrants, some of your people will insist they're already being generous because they give money to the church or non-profit organizations, but they have no desire to actually talk to those people their money goes to help . . . and they can't imagine becoming friends with them! They think you're talking about walking into gang territories where they'll be caught in the middle of a drive-by shooting or a drug deal, or you want them to become a street preacher yelling at people that they're going to hell. So . . . one of the main jobs of a leader who is committed to culture change is to paint a realistic, honest, and attractive picture of what community involvement looks like. As I've said, you already have people who are

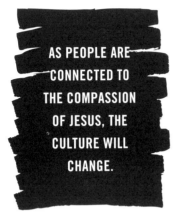

AS PEOPLE ARE CONNECTED TO THE COMPASSION OF JESUS, THE CULTURE WILL CHANGE.

involved in outreach on their own. Showcase these people and let their stories be an example to everyone who has mistaken, negative assumptions. (They may discover some of their friends have been caring for disadvantaged people for years!)

Many church and business leaders say that changing an organization's culture is very difficult. That may be true, but those who claim to follow the God of grace need to move heaven and earth to align their church's culture with the heart of God. As more people in our churches are connected to the compassion of Jesus, the culture will gradually (or maybe radically) change. Most will be thrilled and challenged as they reach out to care for people who are often overlooked, some will feel confused because this kind of outreach isn't at all their experience of church before, and a few—hopefully very few—will think we've lost our minds. Even then, we're in good company. People accused Jesus of being crazy and demon-possessed, and they wondered if the early Christians could really be so loving and generous. Yes, they could and they were . . . but only because they were connected to the heart of God.

MATTHEW 25:34-40

"Then the King will say to those on his right, 'Come, you who are blessed by my Father; take your inheritance, the kingdom prepared for you since the creation of the world. For I was hungry and you gave me something to eat, I was thirsty and you gave me something to drink, I was a stranger and you invited me in, I needed clothes and you clothed me, I was sick and you looked after me, I was in prison and you came to visit me.'

"Then the righteous will answer him, 'Lord, when did we see you hungry and feed you, or thirsty and give you something to drink? When did we see you a stranger and invite you in, or needing clothes and clothe you? [39] When did we see you sick or in prison and go to visit you?'

"The King will reply, 'Truly I tell you, whatever you did for one of the least of these brothers and sisters of mine, you did for me.'"

THINK ABOUT IT

1

What are the temptations to craft our churches according to the preferences of the rich, beautiful, and powerful?

....

....

....

....

....

....

....

2

How does our experience of God's grace reverse the world's values?

....

....

....

....

....

....

....

3

What are some signs our hearts have been melted and molded by a life-changing experience of the grace of God?

....

....

....

....

....

....

....

....

....

....

4

What amazes you about Jesus' interactions with outcasts and misfits?

....

....

....

....

....

....

....

....

....

....

5

What does it mean to
say "graced people
grace people"?

....

....

....

....

....

....

....

....

....

....

6

What would it take for
you to "move heaven
and earth to align your
church's culture with the
heart of God"?

....

....

....

....

....

....

....

....

....

....

JAMES LICK
MIDDLE SCHOOL

I believe every city has a key to it. If you can find the key to your city, you can unlock the opportunity to reach them with the love of Jesus.

PASTOR MARC ESTES
City Bible Church, Portland, Oregon

CHAPTER TWO

CRACKING THE CODE

MAYBE IT SAYS MORE

Maybe it says more about me than I want people to know, but I've always been fascinated with safecrackers. (In movies, think of *The Italian Job* and *Oceans 11, 12,* and *13*.) This is, I believe, the perfect metaphor to describe how we figure out how to engage with our communities. Opening "the safe" of our communities requires us to listen carefully, have a delicate touch, and stay determined when the door doesn't open for a while. If we're persistent, sooner or later we'll crack the code.

How does this happen? Actually, it's not that difficult. We crack the code in our communities by having intentional (and sometimes spontaneous) conversations . . . and listening very, very carefully. In most cases, the people who are already in our churches know the code. They haven't told us only because we haven't asked. We need to pray and ask God to lead us to people who have insights and experience with needy people. They'll be glad to tell us all we need to know.

When God was beginning to give me a vision to care for our community, I asked Him to bring people into my life who could help me. I met with an

Emergency Room nurse and asked her to tell me what patients and their families experience when they come through the ER doors. She told me about the uncertainty and fear they all suffer as the doctors, nurses, and techs jump into action to save a life. This conversation opened my eyes to the trauma people experience every day in the ER, and we discovered ways we could comfort them.

One day, I had lunch with a man who is a probation officer. He and his family were new to our church, and I was just getting to know him. After only a few minutes, however, I realized this was much more than a get-to-know-you and welcome-to-our-church conversation. It was another answer to my prayers! As he talked, the blinders fell off, and I saw things I'd never seen before. I'm sure I had thought newly released prisoners needed time to adjust, but I had no idea about the depth and complexity of the changes required for them and their families.

THIS CONVERSATION OPENED MY EYES TO THE TRAUMA PEOPLE EXPERIENCE EVERY DAY.

Instantly, I realized this man met with people every day who lived on the edge of disaster, and their problems spun out into their families. The probation officer's life was intimately woven into deep, pressing, agonizing needs of ex-cons and those who love them. He knows their pains, their disadvantages, their temptations, their financial and relational struggles, their anger and hopelessness, their desires and dreams. At one point, his eyes lit up and he said, "What thrills me is when I see people on probation—people who are on the knife edge of their futures—make good decisions and begin walking down a path that leads to hope, success, and reconciliation with those they love." He barely finished his sentence before I asked, "Can I help?"

But he wasn't finished. He told me the most discouraging thing about his job is seeing repeat offenders, people who have been given a chance to walk in the light, but they go back to the dark side. Again, I asked, "What can we do to help you with these people?"

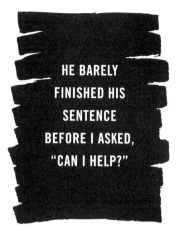

HE BARELY FINISHED HIS SENTENCE BEFORE I ASKED, "CAN I HELP?"

He looked a little surprised that I was so eager to join him in his work. He took out a piece of paper and began writing a list of things we could do. He said, "Here's the most important thing you could do: You could partner with the chaplains in the correctional facilities to provide resources and connections for people who are getting out of prison. You could make their transition much smoother and better."

Of course, before this conversation I already knew prisons existed and people eventually got out, but their lives and situations were nowhere on my radar . . . until I had lunch with a man who was new to our church and who happened to be vitally connected to these individuals and their families. He gave me the names of the chaplains in the prisons, and he introduced me to the leaders of nonprofit organizations that provide job training. He pointed me to halfway houses and drug rehab facilities. We began developing relationships with organizations that could provide clothes, housing, career counseling, and connections with employers who were willing to take a risk to hire ex-cons. We were willing to help in any way we could. One of the organizations asked if we'd host a Christmas party for the ex-cons and their families. After years in prison they had almost forgotten how to celebrate. This network of relationships led to one of the most meaningful and effective ministries of our church.

I can't say it was my brilliant investigative mind that cracked the code in this conversation. I just asked, "What do you do for a living?" When he said he was a probation officer, I said, "Tell me about that." (Pretty profound, don't you think?)

The drug epidemic is especially crippling in the lives of those who deal and use. As we got more involved with ex-prisoners and their families, we realized we had to provide something to help them get out of the quicksand of drug abuse and addiction. We found people with the skills, experience, and heart to run a meeting for alcoholics and drug addicts, and that ministry continues to change lives today. The need to address the drug problem was one more aspect of helping this part of our community.

Another pastor had a similarly surprising conversation that cracked the code. My dear friends John and Leslie Siebeling are pastors at The Life Church in Memphis. In a casual conversation with a teacher, they discovered a lot of children have very little to eat after they leave school on Friday afternoons, so they spend the weekend hungry. The pastors and this teacher came up with the idea of "Backpack Buddies," bags filled with enough good food to last kids through the weekend. As they provided for these kids, more teachers said, "Our kids are going

THIS NETWORK OF RELATIONSHIPS LED TO ONE OF THE MOST MEANINGFUL AND EFFECTIVE MINISTRIES OF OUR CHURCH.

hungry, too." Now, The Life Church and other churches provide weekend meals for children in many different schools across Memphis, and their example has inspired churches in other communities to provide food for kids over the weekends.

When you crack a safe (or so I've heard), you gently turn the dial until you feel the tumbler drop. That's the first number. Then you turn it the other way—gently, carefully, quietly—until you feel the tumbler drop again. That's the next number. You keep doing this until you have enough numbers to open the safe. This means that a single conversation may not give you the complete combination to unlock the needs in your community, but it's part of the code. Sooner or later, you'll have all the numbers you need, and the safe will open to the treasure of people's hearts.

> **" SOONER OR LATER...THE SAFE WILL OPEN TO THE TREASURE OF PEOPLE'S HEARTS. "**

KEEP PRAYING, AND SLOW DOWN

DURING OUR ANALYSIS

During our analysis of our communities, we stay connected to the heart of God through prayer, and as we pray, we watch and listen. When we watch the local news and see a family huddling in the street under a blanket as their mobile home goes up in flames, we don't just flip to the cooking channel and forget those people. We make a call (or several calls if that's what it takes) and ask where these people are staying that night, what school supplies their kids need, and what they need to make it the next day, week, and month before they find a new place to live. We certainly can't fix every problem we see on television, but we can ask God to lead us to care for at least a few individuals and families.

If we pay attention to the local news and overhear conversations at the coffee shop, we'll put faces and voices to the statistics about drug abuse, domestic violence, natural disasters, incarceration numbers, inadequate healthcare, needs of the elderly, homelessness, and on and on. I believe we're so inundated by images and data that we simply can't take it all in. As an instinctive mode of self-protection, we become numb to the tragedies we see and hear about every day. I understand the problem of overload, but we need to trust Jesus to give us His eyes to see and His heart to care for people in need.

Cracking the code begins in prayer, and it continues in prayer. We need God to remind us of the grace that has been poured into our lives, and we need Him to give us direction so we can channel His love and tangible resources where He wants them to go. Our people, too, need our example of prayer. They look to us for leadership and administrative direction as we connect with our communities, but they also need to know that we're continually depending on God for everything we do.

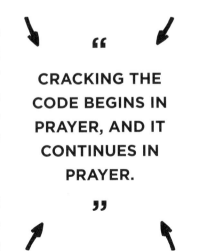

CRACKING THE CODE BEGINS IN PRAYER, AND IT CONTINUES IN PRAYER.

Recently, I realized I was getting ahead of God, so I prayed, "Lord, help me slow down and not move so fast." I had become

> **IF I'M PREOCCUPIED WITH 'ALL THE THINGS I'M DOING FOR GOD,' I WON'T SEE THOSE PRECIOUS MOMENTS WHEN A SMILE MEANS SO MUCH...**

so busy that I was losing my sensitivity to God and awareness of the needs of people. Throughout my day, I have opportunities to be kind to people who need the touch of God's love. If I'm preoccupied with "all the good things I'm doing for God," I won't see those precious moments when a smile, an affirming word, or a simple act of kindness means so much. I've noticed that when I'm in a hurry, people don't tell me about their hopes, fears, sorrow, and joys. But when I'm more relaxed, trusting in God to fulfill all He has called me to be and do, I'm present with the people I see all day. It matters . . . to me, to them, and I suspect, to God. Right after I asked God to help me slow down, I had a casual conversation with a lady at a coffee shop. I guess she sensed I'm a safe person she could trust because she began telling me about her son who is addicted to heroin and is destroying his own life and those he loves. Her heart broke as she told me the story, and mine broke with hers. Slowing down gave me the opportunity to listen, to care, and to help someone in need.

HANDS ON THE DIAL

TO CRACK THE CODE

To crack the code of our communities, we need to put our hands on the dial and begin turning it so we sense the tumbler click into place for each number.

LET ME SUGGEST THESE FIVE SPECIFIC STEPS YOU CAN TAKE.

(1) ENGAGE IN THE DISCOVERY PROCESS.

Dig into the demographic data to get the big picture of who lives around us. The U.S. Census Bureau is a good resource. Their website provides "American FactFinder." Put in the zip code and review the latest data.[1] Other organizations may have vital information you need. Consider The Joshua Survey and Gloo, which is the largest "big data" platform built for churches and other missional organizations to discover important insights about their community. [2]

Then set up appointments to have lunch or coffee with at least a few of these people:

- A guidance counselor at school
- An emergency room nurse
- A police officer, or better, the captain
- Someone who works in child services
- The city manager

---

1   https://factfinder.census.gov/faces/nav/jsf/pages/community_facts.xhtml?src=bkmk

2   To find out more about The Joshua Survey, go to www.JoshuaSurvey.com and for more information about Gloo, go to gloo.us.

- An addiction counselor
- A firefighter
- A social worker
- A community activist
- Agencies that advocate for the elderly or those with disabilities
- Other pastors and church leaders who are serving people in the community

A WEALTH OF INFORMATION IS ONLY A PHONE CALL AND A CUP OF COFFEE AWAY.

At least some of these people are probably men and women of faith, and some may be attending your church. A wealth of information is only a phone call and a cup of coffee away. Carve out plenty of time to meet with these people. Ask simple but direct questions about what they see are the biggest needs in the community. They know people, so they're a rich source of information. Listen carefully, ask follow-up questions to get more details, and write down what you hear. Let them know you take them seriously.

Then, meet with leaders of foundations and organizations that already serve your community. Contact those who lead homeless shelters, food pantries, The Red Cross, The Salvation Army, Centers for Pregnancy, Meals on Wheels, mental health facilities, Hospice, addiction treatment centers, organizations that help women (and sometimes men) who are victims of domestic violence, and counseling centers. Ask them what needs they see and serve, and ask how you and your church might partner with them. Quite often, people in our churches are serving as staff members or volunteers in these organizations, so we already have an open door.

Develop your own set of interview questions as you meet with these people. Some that I often use are very obvious but revealing:

- TELL ME ABOUT YOUR WORK. HOW DO YOU MAKE A DIFFERENCE IN PEOPLE'S LIVES?
- WHAT ARE YOUR BIGGEST CHALLENGES?
- HOW ARE YOU MEETING THOSE CHALLENGES NOW?
- HOW CAN WE PARTICIPATE WITH YOU?

Your demographic analysis and these conversations may take a few weeks or a few months. Be diligent, but don't rush the process. Expect God to bring some specific needs to the surface. You'll almost certainly find more needs than your church can possibly meet, so you'll need wisdom to know where to focus your time and resources. Build a team and rely on them: let the people who are passionate, skilled, and willing to lead help you determine where your focus should be.

② PHONE A FRIEND.

During the entire discovery process, and especially near the end when your ideas are gelling, find someone (and perhaps more than one person) who can answer questions, give you direction, warn you of pitfalls, and be a friend to you as you take steps forward. Don't just find someone who will tell you what you want to hear. Find someone who has been down this

BE DILIGENT, BUT DON'T RUSH THE PROCESS.

YOU DON'T NEED TO REINVENT THE WHEEL. GOD IS ALREADY AT WORK THROUGH YOUR PEOPLE.

road, has made his or her share of mistakes, and can give you spiritual and organizational wisdom—and you need both. This person will encourage your vision, challenge your assumptions, force you to think more clearly, help you plan more effectively, and celebrate your progress.

Most of us have a fair share of apprehension as we launch into this ministry. That's completely normal. It's true: you'll make mistakes, but they aren't the end of the world. You'll make fewer mistakes and less cataclysmic mistakes if you have a friend or two who will give you good advice in the discovery and planning process. And these people will help you learn from any mistakes you make.

FOLLOW FAVOR.

Notice the open doors and the enthusiasm of your people as you step through doors of opportunity. Where do you already see a strong connection between people in your church and the needs in the community? Where are resources already flowing, or how might you tap into some resources you recently discovered? And who is showing initial enthusiasm for this ministry? You don't need to reinvent the wheel. God is already at work through your people. Find how God is using them, and explore how you can bring more resources, passion, and energy to their efforts.

When the leaders of The Life Church realized hundreds of kids were going hungry over the weekends, they met with school officials to ask how they could partner with the school to provide meals for the children. As they talked about their vision, people in the church volunteered time, resources, and administrative talents. Someone wanted to coordinate with the administrations at the schools, several were excited about putting the meals together, and someone else had access to a small delivery truck. It was perfect for taking hundreds of Backpack Buddies to the schools on Friday afternoons. The leaders of The Life Church recognized God's favor, and they simply walked through the doors He was opening.

NOTICE THE OPEN DOORS AND THE ENTHUSIASM OF YOUR PEOPLE AS YOU STEP THROUGH DOORS OF OPPORTUNITY.

 4 FAILURE IS AN OPTION.

I tell pastors this inescapable fact of ministry: if they're really devoted to help their communities, they'll fall flat on their faces from time to time. I'm not advocating disastrous mistakes as a ministry strategy, but engaging in the deepest needs of people inevitably results in plenty of errors and mishaps. There is no doubt, though, that the successes are worth it. Just ask a Texas wildcatter. Oilmen may drill a dozen wells, but if only one of them hits black gold, it's worth it. Our efforts in serving the needs of the people around us have a far higher success rate, but don't be discouraged (or surprised) if you hit a dry hole from time to time. Learn from it and move on.

 5 BUILD PARTNERSHIPS

Before you begin the discovery process, you can probably list a dozen or more agencies and organizations doing good work in your community.

After a few weeks of meeting with people and asking questions, that list will probably double or triple. It's a treasure hunt. If you keep digging and looking, you'll find wonderful, good-hearted people already touching the lives of the poor and disadvantaged. You won't create a partnership with all of them, but it's wise to pool your resources with at least a few of them.

Many of these organizations were founded by Christians—a few only a short time ago, but some many years ago. They may or may not have exactly the same doctrinal stance as you have listed in your bylaws, but learn to overlook relatively minor differences. Of course, a few may hold views that are simply unacceptable to you and your church. Don't make a big deal of it. Just move on. But don't look for arguments. Churches can partner in love with those who have differing beliefs to care for people in their communities. Their relationship doesn't water down what each believes. It only shows the community that helping hurting people is more important than our differences.

When we partner with organizations, we rub shoulders with people from other races, other countries, other languages, and other cultures. In these

HELPING HURTING PEOPLE IS MORE IMPORTANT THAN OUR DIFFERENCES.

interactions, we don't go with an air of superiority that we're the heroes who have come to fix their problems. We're all created in the image of God, and our only standing before Him is by His wonderful grace.

In every stage of the development of this ministry, we learn the importance of listening. I went to a meeting of African-American church leaders in our city. Being the only white guy in the room,

CRACKING THE CODE TO OUR COMMUNITIES

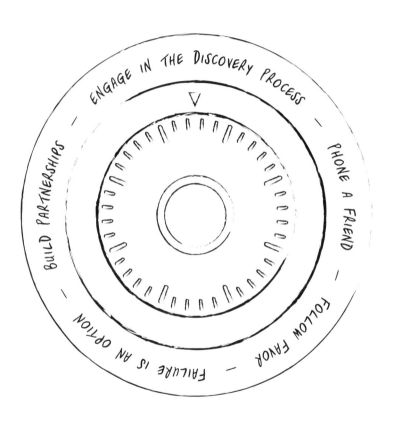

I decided to position myself and listen before I chose to speak. I came to learn that this is a part of serving the needs of others. Being quiet and listening was the best way to show the love of God. After that, we could all be sure we were on the same page, telling others the same message.

Partnerships may be formal or informal. At some point, you may have a presence on the board of a local organization, but at first, providing volunteers and other resources is plenty of participation . . . and it's gratefully accepted.

THREE STAGES

EVERY COMPASSIONATE OUTREACH

Every compassionate outreach ministry begins somewhere. It takes time and attention to build an effective outreach ministry. In the next three chapters, we'll look at three distinct stages of developing this ministry:

STAGE 1: ALL CALL

Pastors and church leaders provide an opportunity for everybody in the church (and I mean *everybody* is invited) to roll up their sleeves and get involved. This event may happen once a year or perhaps once a quarter. Give everyone in your church an easy opportunity to explore ways to use their gifts to help people outside the church. No matter how developed a community ministry may be, the church continues to have All Calls on a regular basis because there are always people new to the church who need and want to get involved.

STAGE 2: CONSISTENT CONNECTIONS

At some point, the leaders crack the code of the community and invest considerable resources to meet a few specific needs. Volunteers usually work with partner organizations, or less frequently, the church creates their own organizations. Small groups begin to form around people's passion to meet needs they see in the community.

STAGE 3: A SUSTAINED SERVE

When we hear the term "Dream Center," we often think of the large churches with millions of dollars invested in facilities and staff who run health clinics, women's shelters, homes for women who have escaped trafficking, and other large and expansive endeavors. Just as the church isn't the building, a Dream Center isn't a building either. It's always about people. The goal of Stage 3 is to create an organized and structured expression of people helping people — a sustained serve in the community. No matter how big or small your church may be, you can have an effective, ongoing, visible ministry that provides resources in your community.

Stage 1 begins the process, but it never ends. Stage 2 continues the process, but it, too, never ends . . . and in fact, a church's presence in the community may take many different forms as more volunteers and resources come onboard. Stage 3 requires more resources and commitment, and of course, it never ends either. The diagram on the following page shows the progression:

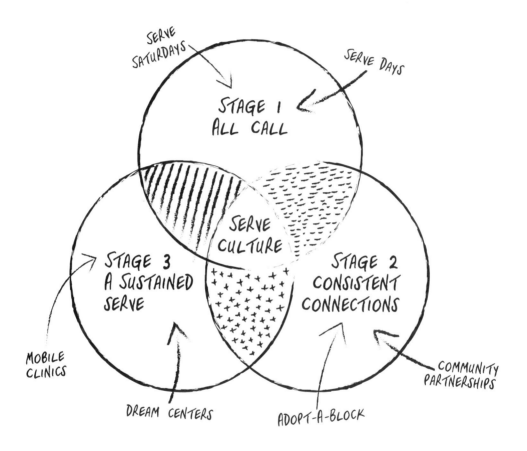

SERVE
SATURDAYS

SERVE DAYS

STAGE 1
ALL CALL

SERVE
CULTURE

STAGE 3
A SUSTAINED
SERVE

STAGE 2
CONSISTENT
CONNECTIONS

MOBILE
CLINICS

DREAM CENTERS

ADOPT-A-BLOCK

COMMUNITY
PARTNERSHIPS

WE'LL DIVE INTO THESE THREE STAGES IN THE FOLLOWING CHAPTERS.

JEREMIAH 22:3-5

This is what the LORD says: Do what is just and right. Rescue from the hand of the oppressor the one who has been robbed. Do no wrong or violence to the foreigner, the fatherless or the widow, and do not shed innocent blood in this place. For if you are careful to carry out these commands, then kings who sit on David's throne will come through the gates of this palace, riding in chariots and on horses, accompanied by their officials and their people. But if you do not obey these commands, declares the LORD, I swear by myself that this palace will become a ruin.

1

Write an initial plan for the discovery process to help you crack the code of how to serve your community.

....

....

....

....

....

....

....

2

Who are some friends (maybe just one) who can help you take steps forward?

....

....

....

....

....

....

....

THINK ABOUT IT

3

What might it look like
to "follow favor" as you
begin or expand
this ministry?

....

....

....

....

....

....

....

....

....

....

4

What happens when
leaders forget that
failure is an option?

....

....

....

....

....

....

....

....

....

....

5

What are some
organizations in your
community where your
people already volunteer?
What are some that you
admire, you already know
the leaders, and might be
a really good fit for
your church?

....

....

....

....

....

....

....

....

....

....

....

....

....

....

....

....

....

....

....

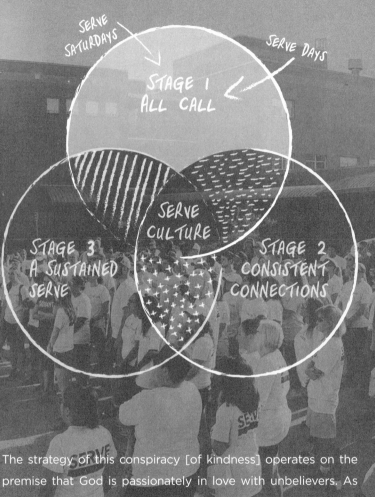

The strategy of this conspiracy [of kindness] operates on the premise that God is passionately in love with unbelievers. As dynamic seeds of kindness are planted in their hearts, the Holy Spirit will pursue them. We are the sowers of those seeds of love. God is the farmer who oversees the entire process.

STEVE SJOGREN
A Conspiracy of Kindness

CHAPTER THREE

STAGE 1: ALL CALL

ONE OF OUR FIRST ACTIVITIES

One of our first activities to serve our community was as simple as it gets: we gave away bottles of water. I don't know what the parallels might be in New England or the Northwest, but in the South, it's hot about nine months of the year—and so humid you'd think you could cut the air with a knife. Actually, the first time or two, we gave away cans of Coke and Diet Coke, but we soon realized thirsty people would rather drink good, pure, cold water.

It didn't take long in our discovery process to realize room temperature water wasn't very attractive to people who were sweating. Hours before we left the church, we had the bottles on ice. If we thought we could give them all out quickly, we took them out of the ice and drove to the part of town where we were distributing them. But if we were going a long way, or if we suspected it would take longer to give out all the water, we kept the water in coolers and hauled them to the streets. We also soon found out that not all coolers are created equal—the ones with wheels save a lot of wear on backs!

> **THE FIRST STEP OF COMMUNITY ENGAGEMENT — FOR A CHURCH, A SMALL GROUP, A FAMILY, OR AN INDIVIDUAL — IS TO WORK TOGETHER...**

People appreciated us giving them a cool drink on a scorching day, but it dawned on us that we were missing an opportunity. We created and printed cards to give people. These included our church name, phone number, website, and a simple message: "We hope this small gift brightens your day. It is a simple way to say God loves you—no strings attached. Let us know if we can help you."

Even with the simplest of strategies, we had to go through a learning curve to get it right. The smiles from those who had a cool drink of water told us we were on the right track. It was the beginning of what we now call a SERVE Day. We invite everybody in the church to participate in acts of kindness, so we issue an "All Call." It's that simple and that big, and it's incredibly effective.

THE FIRST STEP

THE FIRST STEP OF COMMUNITY

The first step of community engagement—for a church, a small group, a family, or an individual—is to work together on a designated day for a few hours to meet specific, tangible needs. At the beginning of our church's history, and still today, we ask everybody in the church to come together on a particular summer Saturday morning. We call it an "All Call" for a "SERVE Day" (or sometimes called "Love Your City Day"). In the weeks before that morning, we contact people and organize resources for a few specific ways people can serve. That morning, we go house to house to visit and pray with people, stand on a street corner to give out bottled water, cut grass at widows' houses, visit nursing homes, paint teachers' lounges at local schools, and many other simple but meaningful tasks.

We encourage small groups to participate together. They know each other well, so they can encourage people to use their gifts. Also, they often have plenty of resources to meet particular needs. Churches that are just starting small groups can use the All Call as a catalyst to start groups. The shared experience of serving gets them off to a great start, deepens their relationships, and gives them meaning beyond the group meetings.

> THE SHARED EXPERIENCE OF SERVING GETS YOUR SMALL GROUPS OFF TO A GREAT START, DEEPENS THEIR RELATIONSHIPS, AND GIVES THEM MEANING BEYOND THE GROUP MEETINGS.

We make sure to have family-friendly options so kids can be involved. We look for opportunities that are high touch so they connect with people. We want everyone to be able to look into the eyes of those they serve. But these days are time-limited. We don't expect families with young children to be out all day.

Christmas is another excellent time for an All Call. Church of the Highlands connects our people with kids and families who don't have resources for gifts at Christmas. Like other organizations that orchestrate toy drives at this time of the year, we talk to teachers and representatives of children's services to identify families in need. We find out the ages and genders of the kids, and we make a list of suggested gift items. We then ask our people to bring unwrapped gifts and wrapping paper to the church, where a team sorts all the items. We set up a "shopping mall" where parents can come to "shop" for their kids so they can give presents on Christmas morning. This makes parents the heroes, not us. This event provides hundreds of people with the chance to serve by sorting toys, displaying them at the mall, wrapping gifts after they're selected, providing hospitality for parents, praying for the event and the parents, loading gifts into cars, and taking care of details. On the day the "mall" is open, our people spend time with the parents who participate. We want to build relationships with them, not just have a transactional exchange. While our members are involved in the event from gift purchase to serving at the event, we always take videos and pictures to capture stories from the day so we can share the big picture of how God used their generosity and kindness.

Celebration Church in Austin, Texas, hosts an annual car prep for single moms, widows, and military wives. This All Call brings together their entire church and provides places for all ages to have a hands-on experience making a difference. Their men's teams take care of oil changes and tune ups, youth teams wash the cars, and women's teams host a pampering zone for guests as they wait on their cars to be finished. The women who are served that day feel loved, and everyone in the church leaves fulfilled knowing they played an important and meaningful role.

Pastors Joe and Danielle Pena and their team launched Relentless Church in Las Vegas at the beginning of 2015. On launch day, they were thrilled that 286 people attended, and they celebrated even more that 22 of them filled out connect cards indicating they had made a decision to follow Christ. For the next several weeks, attendance settled down to just above 100, but by Easter, they were seeing slow but steady growth. Then in June, ARC invited Relentless Church to be part of Serve Day 2015. Pastor Joe recalls, "ARC's invitation to be part of Serve Day proved to be a big win for us because new people who came to Relentless Church during that time were able to connect quickly in a way that fit them. Many loved the idea of getting involved in serving their community, so they came and got connected right away." By mid-July, Relentless Church was averaging nearly 200 in attendance. Instead of seeing a decline in weekly attendance through the summer, they saw a steady increase. Since Serve Day 2015, their attendance has continued to rise. They've outgrown their venue and moved into a bigger one, and they've seen hundreds of people give their hearts to Jesus. The people of the church are thriving and are now "paying it forward," reaching out to others in the same way people reached out to them.

> **THE PEOPLE OF THE CHURCH ARE THRIVING AND ARE NOW "PAYING IT FORWARD," REACHING OUT TO OTHERS IN THE SAME WAY PEOPLE REACHED OUT TO THEM.**

Specific, identifiable wins are important for SERVE Days. The report given the next Sunday in church can show pictures or videos and say things like: "We gave out 3,000 bottles of water. We cut grass and trimmed bushes in 12 yards for elderly people. We sang for and talked with 73 people at a nursing home. We served 225 meals for people who were rebuilding houses. We saw smiles on 42 kids with special needs. We met Mrs. Bertha, Gregory, Quinton and Richard—whose lives are forever changed. We're thrilled God used us to touch so many people!"

If the church has an emphasis on small groups, organize the SERVE Days around group involvement. Coordinate with the group leaders to assign tasks, let them choose from a list of options, or let them create their own

> **GRADUALLY, BY THE PUSH OF US TAKING THE INITIATIVE AND THE PULL OF CIVIC LEADERS ASKING FOR OUR HELP, THE LIFE OF OUR CHURCH BECAME WOVEN INTO THE FABRIC OF THE COMMUNITY.**

SERVE opportunity. You might ask them to provide the resources necessary to complete the task, or the church can provide them. The group's participation strengthens their relationships and gives them a shared memory. Getting them out of a living room and sweating (or singing) together often fosters a deeper level of trust and openness among them.

When a church develops a reputation of combining compassion and creativity, sometimes unexpected resources just show up at the door. Someone once donated a pallet of rat bait, so we had a spontaneous SERVE Day to drive through trailer parks and other neighborhoods to knock on doors and offer rat killer. People were surprised by our offer, but I guarantee you this: they never forgot that moment! We've had a number of tractor-trailers park in front of our church with all kinds of things: bananas, vegetables, lingerie and nightgowns among them.[1] When we said "yes" to the opportunities God sent our way—as bizarre as they may have been—community leaders began to see us as a resource, and they started calling us to help them with events in the city. Gradually, by the push of us taking the initiative and the pull of civic leaders asking for our help, the life of our church became woven into the fabric of the community.

Disaster relief is always an All Call, but it doesn't happen only for a few hours on a Saturday. After a devastating flood, tornado, earthquake, or

---

1   You can read much more about these donations in *Servolution*.

fire, the community needs help for weeks and perhaps even months. In this case, everyone is encouraged to participate, but the effort requires much more organization, time, skills, training, planning, and resources.

THE SIZE OF YOUR CHURCH DOESN'T DICTATE WHETHER YOU HAVE AN ALL CALL

TRY THIS

THE SIZE OF YOUR CHURCH

The size of your church doesn't dictate whether you have an All Call SERVE Day or not, but it determines the scope of activities. Even before the church officially begins, the launch team can begin to build a reputation in the community by having a SERVE Day and caring for people—gladly, effectively, and with no strings attached. People will notice!

THE PLANNING PROCESS IS VERY SIMPLE:

1. Identify a few (maybe three to five) needs in the community. I've already given you some examples of things we've done, but you may have far better ideas of how to involve families to meet specific needs. These tasks can come from conversations with community leaders, or people in your church may have connections with people in need and tell you about them.

2. Select a day that is most convenient, probably at least a month in the future.

3. Spend a few weeks identifying leaders for each task (in a small church you may have only one task, so you might be the leader), gathering

resources, and connecting the leaders with a contact person at the SERVE location when that's important. If your church has small groups, they'll serve together, but there are always people who aren't in groups who want to participate, so plan to offer opportunities for them to be included in serving, too.

THE POINT IS THAT SERVE DAY IS JUST THE BEGINNING.

4. On the morning of SERVE Day, gather everybody together at 8:00 or so. You might serve a quick breakfast. Give them some insights about how to connect with people and live by the Golden Rule. Explain the language of serving. For instance, we don't cram our beliefs down their throats, and we don't even push our church. We're just there to love and serve. If spiritual conversations arise, make sure they're relaxed and wanted. Inspire your people with a vision that their efforts that day will certainly encourage those they serve, and they just might make an eternal difference in the lives of some they meet. Pray for them and send them out. We usually invite people back to eat lunch with us after they serve.

5. At lunch, thank everybody for serving, and ask them to share how God used them that day. You might interview a few people—preferably a diverse group of people—who can articulate their experience that morning. Their stories will resonate with everyone. Thank them for representing Christ to their community, and send them off with a promise that you'll give them another opportunity for a SERVE Day in the future. (We always provide information about ways they can serve every day, not just on SERVE Day. We explain that they can serve

informally through personal acts of kindness, joining an outreach team, starting an outreach-focused small group, or working with a partner organization. The point is that SERVE Day is just the beginning.)

PROJECT IDEAS

THE LIST OF POSSIBILITIES

The list of possibilities for SERVE Days can be limitless. To stimulate your creativity and imagination, look at this list we've posted on our ServeDay website:

First, we ask some important questions:

— WHO IN YOUR NEIGHBORHOOD HAS A NEED? WHAT NEEDS TUG AT YOUR HEART?

— WHAT BUSINESS OR ORGANIZATION WITHIN YOUR SPHERE OF INFLUENCE COULD USE A BLESSING?

— WHAT PROJECT TYPES BEST SUIT YOUR GROUP'S AGES AND ABILITIES? (PRAYER, WORSHIP, TEACHING, PHYSICAL LABOR, ETC.)

We've compiled some ideas to get churches started:

General Ideas

- Host a free garage sale
- Bring free lunches to construction workers and service people in your area
- Hand out free gum at a local park
- Clean up a widow's or single mom's yard
- Give out free sunscreen at a city park

- Give out free bottled water
- Plan a "Back to School Bash" for foster care children. Have free food, games, and a backpack/school supply giveaway
- Give out free donuts and coffee at the bus station or a shopping center
- Host a free car wash
- Provide minor car repairs for elderly, widows and/or single moms
- Kids host a free lemonade stand

Nursing Homes

- Deliver fresh flowers to the residents
- Host a worship service at a nursing home (offer worship, devotions, prayer, and fellowship)
- Throw a "Senior Prom" complete with live music, food, and decorations
- Landscape a flower garden and sitting area for residents
- Clean the windows of residents' rooms inside and outside
- Build birdfeeders and put them outside the windows of residents' rooms
- Have kids make crafts (necklaces, wooden crosses) that can be given to residents
- Distribute sugar-free snacks to residents and employees (check with staff on food restrictions)
- Host an art contest and display residents' paintings (and perhaps set up an auction to sell them)
- Have a tea party
- Help the residents complete care packages for foster kids—this gives them a renewed sense of purpose
- Help residents get dressed up and bring in a professional photographer to have their portraits made

College

- Serve free drinks or snacks at sporting team and band practices
- Give away free mechanical pencils or energy drinks to students
- Host a free picnic in the quad
- Give out free donuts and coffee on the quad
- Help freshmen move into the dorms (moving crews, welcome baskets, care kits, etc.)

Special Needs/Youth Home

- Identify a family with a special needs child and give the family a mom and dad's day out
- Adopt a group home for the day and throw a party for the residents
- Build a ramp for someone who uses a wheelchair
- Organize a field day for a youth group home
- Organize a "fun day" for foster parents
- Do a home or room makeover

Street Outreach

- Serve hot meals for people experiencing homelessness in your community
- Do a community prayer walk and trash clean up
- Host a "Block Party" with free food, games, music, etc. for families
- Renovate a run-down playground or park in the area
- Do a door-to-door grocery giveaway
- Have a "Free Grass Culling" day
- Assemble and distribute hygiene packs
- Walk around and give out free donuts

Hospitals

- Serve free coffee, energy drinks, and snacks to staff and those waiting in the emergency room
- Give out healthy snacks and small blankets to patients of chemotherapy
- Deliver small gifts to patients and families in the children's ward (toys, balloons, stickers, care packages, etc.)
- Conduct prayer visits with patients and those in emergency waiting rooms

Business/Service Organizations/Public Service People

- Wash windows
- Pick up trash in parking lots
- Corral shopping carts to designated spaces
- Cook lunch for your local police or fire station[2]

In our experience, some of the biggest wins include:

- **Projects in local schools**

Many churches meet in schools, so this is a natural fit. Quite often, the schools provide the resources (paint, plants, cleaning supplies, etc.), so usually, there's not much expense for the church or the people serving there. Teacher appreciation activities are also big hits with the administration and teachers.

- **Goody bags for law enforcement officers, EMS, and firefighters.**

It's never a bad idea to build relationships with the men and women who are dedicated to protect you and rescue

---

2   For these and more ideas, go to www.ServeDay.today

you! Come up with creative, tasty, meaningful gifts to show your appreciation for them.

• **Visit nursing homes**

Most nursing homes love to have visitors, especially children, spend time with their residents. A smile, some kind words, and a few minutes of interaction mean the world to them. Come up with some creative activities. Bring in some Nerf guns and watch World War II vets come alive! Refuge Church in Huntsville, Alabama, has even launched an entire nursing home church campus, right in the Alzheimer's unit!

• **"Street kits"**

We've put together bags of essentials for people who are living on the street. The bags include a toothbrush and toothpaste, soap, washcloth, socks, and food items they can carry in their pockets or backpacks. Assembling kits and writing notes of encouragement may be the perfect SERVE opportunity for parents who have smaller children or aren't quite ready to venture to the streets just yet.

• **Free car washes**

These are fun, popular, and highly interactive. Many people can't believe they get something for free, so they're thrilled to come by and get their car washed. Teenagers, college students, and other young adults get to interact with people who drive in for a free wash. Yeah, the washers often get as much soap on them as the cars, but it's all part of the fun environment.

In his book, *Conspiracy of Kindness*, Pastor Steve Sjogren describes how their church advertises a "$1 Car Wash," but they give the dollar back

TO BUILD A CULTURE OF SERVING, PEOPLE NEED TO BE EMPOWERED TO LEAD.

to the drivers when their car is clean. This is another way to surprise people with kindness.

After a few SERVE Days, you will have identified people in your church who have very useful skills. At Church of the Highlands, we developed a Skilled Projects Team who can do car repairs and home repairs—carpentry, electrical work, plumbing, masonry, landscaping, etc.—for single moms, widows, elderly people, and others who need our help. By this time, you also probably have working relationships with nonprofit organizations, and partnerships are developing. These relationships focus your efforts and multiply the impact.

STAGE 1 PRINCIPLES

IN OUR EXPERIENCE

In our experience with All Calls and SERVE Days, we've learned a lot of important lessons. Let me summarize the essential ones we've learned:

 1 PICK THE RIGHT LEADERS.

To build a culture of serving, people need to be empowered to lead. They need to learn that they are the church, and it's not up to the church staff to figure everything out and make everything happen.

In a small church or even one that hasn't opened its doors yet, the pastor may be the only team leader. If you have small groups, ask the group leaders to lead teams, and be sure to provide leaders for people who aren't in groups but show up on Saturday morning. Meet with the leaders before SERVE Day to inform them, let them choose their venue, provide resources, and answer all their questions.

But don't force people to lead a project they're not passionate about. For instance, if you don't have a leader who wants to lead a carwash, scrap the carwash until the right leader comes along.

2 FIND THE RIGHT SEASON.

Make sure the date of the SERVE Day fits the timing of the church calendar—and don't forget to look at the community calendar, too. We have our primary SERVE Day in the summer when college students are home and can participate, the calendar isn't as full, and people feel comfortable being outside. We schedule ours in July. (In Alabama, you would never have a SERVE Day on a Saturday afternoon in the fall because so many people are watching college football!)

It might be wise to have only one SERVE Day the first year. Plan it well, organize your people, secure your resources, and make it wonderful. But the next year, you might have one a quarter, or have special SERVE Days at Easter and Christmas. Today, we have a SERVE Day on the first Saturday of every month, and these are largely led by our small groups who have developed partnerships with nonprofits in the city, but it started with one All Call for a SERVE Day in Year 1. The movement has grown: today, churches on many continents participate in a worldwide SERVE Day in July.

You can only expand as fast as you develop an infrastructure of leadership, resources, and partnerships. It's more important to provide wonderful experiences for your people and the people they serve than to expand rapidly. Don't "overpromise and under deliver." And by the way, it's not a bad thing for your people to love serving so much they can't wait for the next one!

 ### FIND ACTIVITIES THAT ARE APPROPRIATE FOR FAMILIES.

In an All Call, you're not organizing activities that require a lot of skills and training. Set up events that can easily involve families. Obviously, little babies may not go out for several hours, but many parents want to take their infants to the safe, easy activities. The children and teenagers will have wide eyes, open hearts, and tons of questions. You're giving them and their parents opportunities to step into the lives of people in need and provide real resources, and they're doing it together. Young and old can be involved in block parties, putting goody bags together and taking them to the police officers and firefighters, visiting in nursing homes, and many other valuable connections.

 ### PICK A FEW ACTIVITIES.

Start small, and choose events that have plenty of low hanging fruit—easy to interact and genuinely helpful. We've given you plenty of ideas. Pick just a few.

 ### PLAN EFFECTIVELY.

It's important to provide the resources necessary for the events to go really well. If you're hosting a car wash, make sure you have plenty of hoses, nozzles, buckets, sponges, soap, signs, and towels . . . and connections to several faucets. Again, the goal isn't to blanket the city with volunteers; it's to create a few, excellent, meaningful connections between your people and the people they serve.

 CELEBRATE WELL.

One of the most important elements of SERVE Day is when people come back to have lunch and share their stories. Work hard to make this a meaningful celebration. The encouraging responses to the stories validate people and encourage them do it again and again. Show pictures and videos of the event, and make everyone a hero. Use social media to let the world know how God has worked in those precious hours.

As the leader of SERVE Day, look for where the magic happens. It won't happen in every activity, but it'll happen in many of them. It's the intersection of the needs of the community, the quality of your leaders, the excellence of your resources, the passion of your volunteers, and the results of your planning and preparation. It takes work—maybe more work than you've imagined—but it's well worth every bit of effort you put into it. You're creating a new culture of love, kindness, and sacrifice, and you're proclaiming to your town or city that Jesus cares for them in tangible ways.

> **"**
>
> **MAGIC HAPPENS AT THE INTERSECTION OF THE NEEDS OF THE COMMUNITY, THE QUALITY OF YOUR LEADERS, THE EXCELLENCE OF YOUR RESOURCES, THE PASSION OF YOUR VOLUNTEERS, AND THE RESULTS OF YOUR PLANNING AND PREPARATION.**
>
> **"**

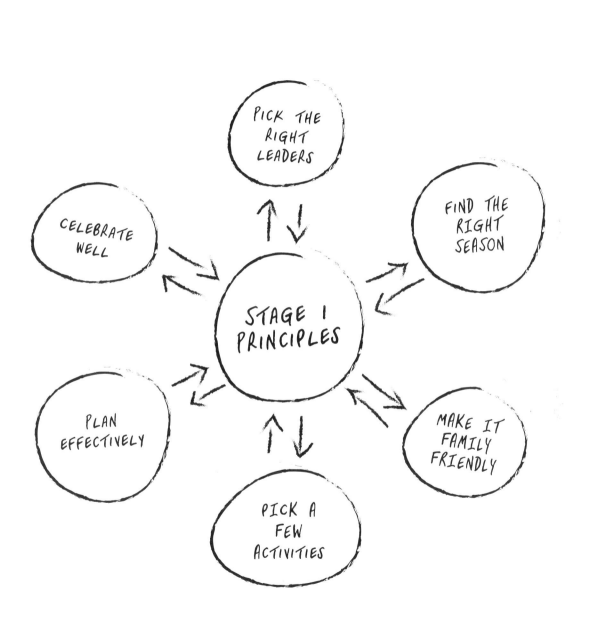

———

JOB 31:16-23

"If I have denied the desires of the poor
   or let the eyes of the widow grow weary,
if I have kept my bread to myself,
   not sharing it with the fatherless—
but from my youth I reared them as a father would,
   and from my birth I guided the widow—
if I have seen anyone perishing for lack of clothing,
   or the needy without garments,
and their hearts did not bless me
   for warming them with the fleece from my sheep,
if I have raised my hand against the fatherless,
   knowing that I had influence in court,
then let my arm fall from the shoulder,
   let it be broken off at the joint.
For I dreaded destruction from God,
   and for fear of his splendor I could not do such things."

———

THINK ABOUT IT

1

Have you ever been involved in any kind of all-church activity to reach out and serve people in the community? If so, how did it go? What worked well and what needed some adjustments?

....
....
....
....
....
....
....

2

When would be a good time of year for your SERVE Day? What makes this time work for your church?

....
....
....
....
....
....
....

3

Look at the list of possible activities in this chapter. Which ones look the most attractive? How will you sift through the options and come up with the ones that work for you?

....
....
....
....
....
....
....
....
....
....

4

How will you select leaders for the teams that go out on SERVE Day?

....
....
....
....
....
....
....
....
....
....

5

What will make this event a huge win for your people? How will you highlight and celebrate those wins?

....

....

....

....

....

....

....

....

....

....

....

....

....

....

....

....

....

....

....

....

....

STAGE 1
ALL CALL

SERVE
CULTURE

STAGE 3
A SUSTAINED
SERVE

STAGE 2
CONSISTENT
CONNECTIONS

COMMUNITY
PARTNERSHIPS

ADOPT-A-BLOCK

If a person has grasped the meaning of God's grace in his heart, he will do justice. If he doesn't live justly, then he may say with his lips that he is grateful for God's grace, but in his heart he is far from him. If he doesn't care about the poor, it reveals that at best he doesn't understand the grace he has experienced, and at worst he has not really encountered the saving mercy of God. Grace should make you just.

TIMOTHY KELLER

Generous Justice

CHAPTER FOUR

STAGE 2:
CONSISTENT CONNECTIONS

LET ME GIVE YOU TWO EXAMPLES

Let me give you two examples of how a Stage 1 temporary effort became consistent connections in serving our community. Both of them revolve around a leader having an idea, which became a vision, and then led to bold, concerted action.

When I was a pastor in Baton Rouge, one of our first acts of serving our community was a Christmas party for single moms. Our church was very small, and we had a couple of these ladies in our little congregation. Trish Freeman had been a single mom who had recently gotten married. After church one day in the late fall, she said in passing, "You know, Pastor Dino, we ought to do something for the single moms in our area. They often feel left out at Christmas. Can we have a party for them?"

Instantly, I knew who should orchestrate this effort. I told her, "Yeah, you should lead it! We'll have a party for them here at the church."

Trish's wheels started turning. She told me she wanted us to have a Santa Claus for the kids, some delicious food, games, and some gifts for the

A STAGE 1 EVENT BECAME A STAGE 2 ONGOING MINISTRY.

moms and their kids. We had the season, and we picked a date. Trish was our leader with a plan, and we started gathering resources. We made an announcement at the church, and before long, six moms signed up to come. A man in our church called me and said, "Pastor, my mother was a single mom. Tell me how much the party is going to cost. I'll write you a check." Then he said, "There's only one condition: can I come?"

How could I say "no"? I told him, "Sure, you can come!"

We had the party, and it was a huge success. Everyone had a blast! The moms and kids felt wonderfully loved. The magic had happened. Almost as soon as the party was over, Trish told me, "Pastor, I bet we could form a small group with the women who came to the party." There wasn't any "we" to it—Trish started the group. Out of the grace she had found in Christ, she loved these women and their children, and she had a tremendous impact on their lives . . . and she inspired my vision for what God might do if we're available to show a little of His kindness to others.

A Stage 1 event became a Stage 2 ongoing ministry: a small group for single moms that welcomed moms from all over the community. Trish understood their struggles, and she was a true friend to them. Many of the women who heard about the small group and joined also began attending our church. The network of love and support was growing because of Trish's leadership. In the next few years, other caring women became leaders, and this ministry grew to 20, then 30, and then 40. In the warmth and support of the groups, these moms didn't feel as isolated or ashamed, as helpless or hopeless. They knew they had a place where they were loved and supported. As the moms kept coming, Trish needed help to care for all of them, and the ministry expanded. That's how an overflow of love attracts and transforms people.

From that moment, we began looking for the next need and the next opportunity to serve people in our community. Our passion to care for those in need snowballed from there.

OUR PASSION TO CARE FOR THOSE IN NEED SNOWBALLED FROM THERE.

The second example is an outreach led by Helen James. She had taught in our local schools in Birmingham for decades. After she retired and began serving with us in the community, she explained that we could have a tremendous impact on the kids in our schools and their families. With her experience and insights, she was able to tell us dozens of things we could do to help. The first need she pointed out was that most of the kids' moms were working, so they weren't available to be homeroom moms. (And some of the moms were in jail, on drugs, or absent from the home for other reasons.) These kids needed surrogate homeroom mothers. We were able to find women in our community who were thrilled to be homeroom moms, and they found plenty of resources for the teachers and students—for regular classroom activities and for special events like Christmas decorations and parties. The homeroom mothers brought supplies like highlighters and paper towels, and they decorated the room for each season of the year. They became a resource and a friend to the teachers where they served.

Before long, Helen helped us identify another set of needs in these schools. We got involved in booster clubs and sports teams, bought uniforms for clubs and teams, led teacher appreciation events, provided much-needed supplies for the teachers, and many others activities. If these small groups and homeroom moms hadn't provided these resources, the kids and teachers would have gone without them. Helen became a switchboard to connect our small groups with the needs in the classrooms, and it was magnificent. The groups adopted a teacher, a team, or a club, and they built relationships as they provided encouragement and resources. Because of Helen's vision, leadership, and compassion, we had consistent connections in our schools with teachers and students who desperately needed our care and resources. The teachers were relieved to have this support, the kids got attention and resources they wouldn't have received otherwise, and our volunteers realized their time and love were making a tremendous difference. Everybody won!

ORGANIC GROWTH

From the many activities a church might do on SERVE Day, a few capture the hearts of a leader or two. They come away from the day saying, "This was great, but it's not enough. We're not done yet. These people need more from us . . . these people need more from me!" These leaders own the specific vision of compassion, and they can't let it go until they find the people and resources to make it happen. Sometimes, these efforts also have an end date. After a SERVE Day, a leader may have a vision to build a playground for a neighborhood that has no place for kids to play. It may take weeks or months to find land, get permits, secure the building materials, and enlist people to come on four or five Saturdays to complete the job. But many other times, God moves someone to create a small group like Trish and the single moms, or to create an ongoing presence like Helen enlisting volunteers to serve in the schools. These leaders and volunteers are living out their God-given calling . . . maybe a calling they had never tapped into before they became aware of the need. Meeting these needs gives them a renewed sense of purpose and a fresh insight on their purpose in God's kingdom.

The transition from Stage 1 to Stage 2 seems to happen naturally and organically, but it also takes sensitivity and planning. Leaders need to watch and listen to see which activities on SERVE Days "stick" and become a consistent connection. Excitement and momentum propels individuals and groups to stay involved, to do more, to make even more of a difference. Some people—not everybody, but some—are moved to have a deeper, longer impact on those they met on SERVE Day.

From my observations in leading outreach ministry for many years, I think about ten percent of a church body has a true heart to serve. Everybody is called to serve, but these few live to serve and love to serve. They get up every day thinking about abandoned children, the sick and the elderly, prisoners, single moms, addicts, widows, and immigrants. These compassionate people usually become the leaders of Stage 2 ongoing ministries in the community. They are the ones who make the additional phone calls, set up appointments with organizations who might become partners, recruit volunteers and organize their efforts. A "free market" small group strategy encourages this kind of involvement. When you create a culture

WATCH AND LISTEN TO SEE WHICH ACTIVITIES ON SERVE DAYS "STICK" AND BECOME A CONSISTENT CONNECTION.

of entrepreneurial thinking and actions among group leaders, your job isn't to drum up enthusiasm, but to celebrate their enthusiasm. You can then say "yes" to most ideas, and you can empower people to step out and lead in an area of their passions.

Out of these ten percent, perhaps one in ten of them feels called to devote his or her life to the causes of the poor and needy. I hope these projections don't discourage you. In fact, it's encouraging to realize you'll have some dedicated, enthusiastic partners! This observation of engagement explains why only a few people get really excited about ongoing ministries of serving the poor in your community. Treasure them. Resource them. Celebrate them. And don't let them burn out!

In Stage 2, your job is identifying the ten percent of men and women whose hearts beat for those in need. They become the tip of the spear as you build strong, loving, consistent ministries to care for overlooked or disadvantaged people in your community. Don't push, and don't set unrealistic goals. Be a gardener who nourishes the growth of compassion and patiently waits to pick the fruit. If you push too hard, you'll run the risk of hardening the hearts of people who can only serve the poor if their hearts are shaped by God's grace and compassion.

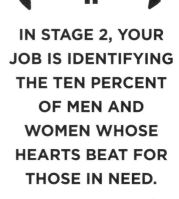

IN STAGE 2, YOUR JOB IS IDENTIFYING THE TEN PERCENT OF MEN AND WOMEN WHOSE HEARTS BEAT FOR THOSE IN NEED.

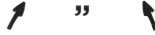

Stage 1 is mostly task-oriented and episodic—half a day once or a few times a year. Stage 2 is the development of ongoing relationships, perpetual touch, a continuous

> **STAGE 2 IS THE DEVELOPMENT OF ONGOING RELATIONSHIPS, PERPETUAL TOUCH, A CONTINUOUS PRESENCE.**

presence. Like Trish's small group for single moms or Helen's coordination of homeroom moms and other efforts in the schools, in Stage 2 we're saying, "We're here, and we're not going away. You can count on us. We want to be your friends, your supporters, and your resources."

One of the most effective, ongoing efforts has been our involvement in neighborhoods. A leader and small group have taken initiative to "adopt" a few blocks or a whole neighborhood, taking groceries to people who can't afford them or can't get out to shop, providing activities for children, and hosting block parties a few times a year. Every week, we pack bags full of groceries and go house to house to see if the people there need something to eat. Before long, the pattern becomes clear: some people need our help as often as we can come by, but others won't even come to the door to talk with us. We're glad to help anyone who needs our assistance. We started this effort in two neighborhoods, and now we're in ten. At this point, we offer groceries every Saturday, but we rotate the neighborhoods where we deliver them, and the volunteers who pack the bags and those who distribute them rotate, too. A volunteer may serve only once a month, and a neighborhood may get grocery deliveries every three weeks. Still, this frequency gives us an ongoing presence in these disadvantaged neighborhoods.

We've created small groups for people who struggle with addictions, groups for the struggling family members of those people, and groups for other people whose lives are out of control and falling apart. We partner with nonprofits to provide volunteers and resources, such as a shelter for women who are escaping sex trafficking, Meals on Wheels, Centers for Pregnancy, and other organizations in the community. People from Healing Place Church have volunteered to care for patients in cancer treatment centers and nursing homes. People who sit for hours hooked up to chemo already feel terrible, and the chemo makes them feel even worse. It doesn't take much for us to show up, to sit with them, offer to read to them or pray for them, and bring them something good to eat. This ministry became so important that Healing Place Church now includes a budget item for snacks for the cancer treatment center. When people from the church show up, everybody smiles . . . and feels loved. This ministry has become a daily affair. I guess there are enough people who have suffered through chemo (or have family members who have) that they want to be there for others going through the same grueling experience. God uses our experiences of suffering to deepen our compassion for others.

SOMETIMES, OUR PEOPLE SHOW UP AT THE MOST VULNERABLE MOMENTS IN SOMEONE'S LIFE.

Sometimes, our people show up at the most vulnerable moments in someone's life. For instance, a member of our church who is a nurse in the Neonatal ICU at a local hospital realized parents sit for hours desperately hoping their child will make it through another day. She enlisted some tenderhearted people who have experienced their own tough times to visit in the waiting room of the NICU once a week to see if any of the parents want to talk. (Of course, those who care for people in this kind of need should be vetted and trained so they will be sensitive to the hopes and fears of these parents, but their presence can mean everything to moms and dads who are struggling to hang on to hope.) After a while, one of our people realized these parents stayed at the hospital all the time and never had time to wash their clothes. We then added the service of washing their clothes so moms and dads could at least feel a little fresher as they waited.

WORKING WITH LOCAL MINISTRIES REVEALS UNMET NEEDS IN THE COMMUNITY AND PROVIDES AN OPPORTUNITY FOR PEOPLE TO FIND THEIR PURPOSE.

In every community, you'll find nonprofit organizations who would love to have a church partner with them to provide caring volunteers and resources. Consistent connections require committed people and key partnerships. It's our privilege to work shoulder to shoulder with these outstanding organizations. Often, working with local ministries reveals unmet needs in the community and provides an opportunity for people to find their purpose. When we began working with a food ministry, sorting and distributing food, we uncovered another need. One of our leaders recognized people we were serving needed even better nutrition. She started a garden so we could give away fresh vegetables. Today, we have a whole team of people serving in the garden . . . which is now more like a farm.

Let me warn you though: If you aren't going to be committed and consistent, don't promise more than you can deliver. Hurting people already don't trust very easily, so one of the most important services we can provide is trustworthiness. If you say you'll be there, be there.

If a church sponsors a food truck that consistently delivers groceries in a neighborhood, they'll often see three generations of people come out to greet them. They don't just know the sound of the truck coming down the street; they also know the volunteers who show up time and time again to care for them. When they receive a bag of food, they hug their friends who have built a relationship with them over many months.

Of course, as we're involved in relationships, we find out about particular needs. We learn someone has cancer and needs a brace fixed to the tub so she can get in and out of the bath more easily. We donated $300 for the equipment and sent someone from our Skilled Projects Team to install it. Problem solved. Mission accomplished. Individual blessed.

Quite often, the needs and the opportunities to meet those needs evolve. As people step in to care, they often realize another need hasn't been obvious until that moment. Interactions with people in need show us another family, another individual, or an entire community that needs substantial help.

When we began our outreach efforts in Baton Rouge, it was entirely event driven, and I was in charge of virtually all of it. It was fun and meaningful, but it was always limited to my capacity. At Church of the Highlands, we've learned that we can multiply our effectiveness and resources by asking small groups to take ownership of tasks on SERVE Day, and if they see a need that requires consistent connections, they can shift their commitment into Stage 2. The group leader (or someone in the group) organizes and

> INTERACTIONS WITH PEOPLE IN NEED SHOW US ANOTHER FAMILY, ANOTHER INDIVIDUAL, OR AN ENTIRE COMMUNITY THAT NEEDS SUBSTANTIAL HELP.

coordinates the people, time, and essential resources to have a presence wherever they feel called. On church-wide SERVE Days, we often send more people to participate with them for a short-term outreach, but the leader and the group have ongoing responsibility with the nonprofit partner, the agency, or the neighborhood.

STAGE 2 PRINCIPLES

Leadership, commitment, and consistency are the hallmarks of Stage 2. Let me reiterate the principles that make this stage work.

(1) IDENTIFY PARTNERS.

For a partnership with a nonprofit to work, we have to *find* the right people, and we have to *be* the right people. Ongoing, consistent connections won't happen without a leader having a vision and enlisting passionate, dedicated people and resources to make it happen week after week. The nature of the work also needs to be sustainable. Either our church or the leader needs to create the system to make it happen, or more probably, the leader builds a relationship with a nonprofit which already has a system in place. We can be partners in one of two ways: we can support activities the organization is already doing, or we can fill in gaps to meet needs that aren't being addressed.

> "LEADERSHIP, COMMITMENT, AND CONSISTENCY ARE THE HALLMARKS OF STAGE 2."

> **THEY'VE LEARNED TO ASK PEOPLE IN CITY GOVERNMENT, "HOW CAN WE SERVE YOU?"**

Pastors Jonathan Wiggins and Samuel Brum of REZ Church in Loveland, Colorado, are leading their people to partner with 50 agencies in their city and around the world. The church's mission statement is "To raise up life-giving followers of Jesus who touch the world with God's love." Through their work with partners, they're helping to provide food and clothing for over 1,000 orphans, they've seen many women freed from trafficking, and through the Jerusalem Institute of Justice, lawmakers in the Middle East are passing legislation to hold nations accountable for human rights violations. In every partnership, they provide tangible relief, but these efforts are also to "disarm the hearts of people to hear the gospel, because that's where real rescue happens."

One of the best pieces of advice they've received came from Pastor Matthew Barnett at the LA Dream Center. They wanted to build credibility with the local Loveland City Council, so he told them to buy a bag of asphalt and to take it and a shovel to the next meeting. When someone complains about potholes, they could say, "We represent REZ Church, and we'll take care of that!" The church can connect some of their resources to the needs of the city government, but only as the city leaders perceive the needs. They don't jump in where they're not wanted. They've learned to ask people in city government, "How can we serve you?" Then they listen carefully and become partners with the city. They've seen that when they honor authority, God will raise them up.[1]

② THE GOAL MUST BE COMPELLING AND REALISTIC.

WHEN THEY HONOR AUTHORITY, GOD WILL RAISE THEM UP.

Some people are motivated by a numerical goal, but most are driven by relationships. A good leader uses both to paint a picture of what success looks like. He might say, "We want to provide three people and a platter of snacks at one cancer treatment center every week this year, and we want to have meaningful conversations with at least ten patients each time." Almost always, the partner organizations have defined very clear goals, and it's our privilege to help them reach them.

③ PROVIDE ADEQUATE RESOURCES.

On SERVE Day, small groups take ownership of particular projects, partnerships, and relationships, and they or the nonprofit partners often provide all the resources they need. The church provides resources for teams of volunteers who aren't in groups yet. Also, when the teams go out and someone discovers a need that isn't being met, the church often provides the funds for the particular need. It's our commitment and our joy to help whenever possible.

---

1   From a webinar: https://www.youtube.com/watch?v=S7DWjm4WKSA&t=1s

At Church of the Highlands, small groups provide the resources for their SERVE Days and other community outreach activities. This strategy keeps virtually all of the ongoing, Stage 2, outreach activities in the realm of small groups.

INSTILL A SENSE OF DIGNITY.

When people are hungry, we feed them. When their homes are washed away, we find them a place to live. As the hands and feet of Jesus, we want to meet needs wherever we find them, but we also need to be wise: if all we do is provide relief, we run the risk of creating a dependent relationship with people we help. In *Generous Justice*, Tim Keller identifies three levels of involvement: relief, development, and social reform. He explains:

> Relief is direct aid to meet immediate physical, material, and economic needs. . . . [Development] means giving to an individual, family, or entire community what they need to move beyond dependency on relief into a condition of economic self-sufficiency. . . which is far more time consuming, complex, and expensive than relief . . . including education, job creation and training, job search skills, and financial counseling. Social reform moves beyond the relief of immediate needs and dependency and seeks to change the conditions and social structures that aggravate or cause that dependency. [2]

These three levels correspond to our three stages of community outreach. Stage 1 is the first and easiest connection, but if we stop there, we fail to help people acquire the ability to be self-sufficient, have a greater sense of self-respect, and provide for themselves and their families.

---

2   Timothy Keller, *Generous Justice* (New York: Dutton, 2010), pp. 112–126.

(It's the principle of teaching people to fish instead of just giving them a fish.) In Stage 2, we're doing more than relief; we're providing assistance to help people take steps to build a successful, meaningful life. In *When Helping Hurts*, authors Steve Corbett and Brian Fikkert explain that well-intended but unwise efforts can produce short-term relief but long-term dependence. In our planning, we need to

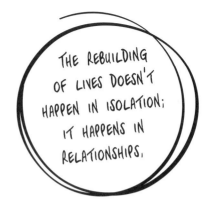

always think about how our care for people instills dignity and offers them an opportunity to rebuild their lives.[3] The rebuilding of lives doesn't happen in isolation; it happens in relationships, so it's important to involve people in every aspect of the church, especially small groups.

As we've seen, the church's role isn't a hit-and-run strategy; it's to transform the community by shaping education, housing, relationships between the poor and the government, and even enacting laws and codes that help people rise out of bondage to poverty, abuse, and drugs. We do all this in the name of Christ, with the life-changing message of Christ, to touch hearts for Christ, so people gladly follow Christ. First to last, it's all about Him.

---

3   I encourage leaders of outreach ministries to read *When Helping Hurts* by Steve Corbett and Brian Fikkert (Chicago: Moody Publishers, 2014).

IDENTIFY PARTNERS

THE GOAL MUST BE COMPELLING AND REALISTIC

STAGE 2 PRINCIPLES

INSTILL A SENSE OF DIGNITY

PROVIDE ADEQUATE RESOURCES

ANYBODY, ANYWHERE ▰▰▰▰▰

THE STAGES OF COMMUNITY

The stages of community outreach operate in any culture and in every country. Of course, leaders have to adapt the principles, and they often find very different needs than we face. In Lima, Peru, Pastor Robert Barriger pursued outreach in a local slum. His people noticed people in wheelchairs who were having great difficulty getting through the ruts and over the debris on the streets. In addition, many of the wheelchairs had rusted because people were out in the rain so often. Robert and his team brainstormed until they found a solution. They designed and patented a plastic wheelchair with larger tires that's much more mobile in rough terrain. Their invention has revolutionized the lives of the crippled people in the slum.

Pastor Robert's people noticed the need when they held a SERVE Day, a Saturday outreach in the slum. Thousands of people had seen people in wheelchairs struggle to move, but Pastor Robert's team noticed and cared enough to come up with a creative solution. They raised the money to design, manufacture, and distribute thousands of wheelchairs to people in need.

> **LOVE AND GENEROSITY HAS OPENED DOORS TO REVEAL MORE NEEDS SO THEY CAN PROVIDE MORE SERVICES.**

And the truckloads of wheelchairs keep on coming. Their invention has given the church consistent connections in the slum, and as always, their love and generosity has opened doors to reveal more needs so they can provide more services. The church is seen as a beloved, valued, trusted part of the community.

Stage 2 is where the magic that happens on SERVE Day becomes an integral part of the life of the church and the community. Leaders are stirred to make a difference, to meet needs they've uncovered, and their passion inflames the hearts of the people in their groups. Together, they devote time and energy, and they build relationships with partner organizations. As they get involved in the lives of the people they serve, two crucial things happen: they inevitably uncover more (and often even more complex) problems that beg to be solved, and they experience the unmitigated joy of knowing they're making a difference in the lives of moms and dads, their kids, and their extended families. When large numbers of people in your church truly know they are the hands and feet of Jesus, watch out: amazing things are already happening, and even more is about to happen!

DEUTERONOMY 15:7-8

If anyone is poor among your fellow Israelites in any of the towns of the land the LORD your God is giving you, do not be hardhearted or tightfisted toward them. Rather, be openhanded and freely lend them whatever they need.

1

Describe how an event-driven All Call can expose needs, leadership, partnerships, and commitment to become Stage 2 consistent connections in the community.

....

....

....

....

....

....

....

2

What are some ways you can identify the ten percent of your people who live and love to care for others?

....

....

....

....

....

....

....

THINK ABOUT IT

3

Why are small groups
a natural fit for Stage
2 leadership and
involvement?

....
....
....
....
....
....
....
....
....
....

4

What are some
organizations in your
community that might
be a good fit for
"consistent connections"
and partnership with
people in your church,
and particularly, at least
some of your small
groups?

....
....
....
....
....
....
....
....
....
....

5

What would you expect to see as the transformative impact of Stage 2 engagement—in the lives of the people in the community and in the lives of people in your church?

....

....

....

....

....

....

....

....

....

....

....

....

....

....

....

....

....

....

....

....

STAGE 1
ALL CALL

SERVE
CULTURE

STAGE 3
A SUSTAINED
SERVE

STAGE 2
CONSISTENT
CONNECTIONS

MOBILE
CLINICS

DREAM CENTERS

Hope

Don't reinvent the wheel. Look around at where God's hand is already moving and go be a part of it or support it.

CHRIS HODGES

CHAPTER FIVE

STAGE 3:
A SUSTAINED SERVE

AT SOME POINT

At some point, the consistent connections churches build with partner organizations may become something more—a recognized, permanent presence providing outstanding care to people in need. This is the third stage in the progression of compassion. Some churches call this presence "a Dream Center." We call it "a sustained serve."

Pastor Matthew Barnett is a dear friend and a personal hero. When he went to Los Angeles in 1994 to start a church, he began to observe the needs of the community. As he prayed and planned, he realized God didn't want a typical church. God led him to move beyond the walls of the building so the church would be woven into the fabric of the community. In this way the people of the church could be the hands, the feet, and the voice of Jesus— all day every day. Today the LA Dream Center ministers to a wide range of people in need, including drug addicts, unwed mothers, women who have been freed from trafficking, gang members, people experiencing homelessness, veterans, those with HIV/AIDS, prisoners, newly released ex-cons, and many other groups of people. Around the country today, there are more than 200 expressions of a church's sustained serve.

WHEN WE CONSIDER STAGE 3 OF A CHURCH'S COMMUNITY OUTREACH PLAN, WE NEED TO KEEP TWO THINGS IN MIND: TIMING AND SCALE.

When pastors and church leaders hear the term "Dream Center," they may think of the ones that are established by large churches that have raised millions, hired outstanding staff, and enlisted a host of passionate, skilled volunteers. When leaders visit these facilities or hear about them, they often instantly think, *Well, that's great, but we certainly can't do anything like that!* If that's your response, I would encourage you to think again.

When we consider Stage 3 of a church's community outreach plan, we need to keep two things in mind: timing and scale. None of these 200 Stage 3 expressions appeared in a flash. They are all the product of years of engagement, planning, and growth. In other words, these churches didn't get to Stage 3 without going through Stages 1 and 2! And scale is important. Large churches can plan and pull off grand programs, but smaller churches can create their own versions of a sustained serve. Stage 3 isn't only for large churches; it's for any church in which Stage 2 has surfaced glaring needs that require a facility, staff, and volunteers to adequately care for people.

TIMING

First, let me address the issue of timing by using our church's process. As we've seen, Helen James was leading our efforts to connect volunteers and resources to local schools. She enlisted women to be surrogate home-room moms, and she asked many others to contribute classroom supplies, uniforms, and other equipment to the schools. Helen and the women who served with her became beloved fixtures in those schools. Stage 2 was alive and thriving under her leadership.

During this time, our pastor, Chris Hodges, had a conversation with a doctor, Robert Record, who attended our church. Dr. Record shared his heart for the people in a disadvantaged neighborhood. In his practice, he took special care to see people who couldn't afford to see him, but that wasn't enough for him; he wanted to practice medicine among "the least of these." Chris instantly realized our church could provide resources to fulfill this vision.

Commercial real estate research showed that the Jefferson County Health Department was closing its doors. The building was constructed as a medical clinic so it wouldn't need major renovations. Also, the clinic happened to be across the street from one of the schools where Helen and her team focused much of their attention. Dr. Record and Helen met with a local schoolboard member over lunch to share with her their vision to serve the community. As soon as they finished, the schoolboard official took them to meet the high school principal. By the time Dr. Record and Helen left the principal's office, the vision had found a home and a real partnership had formed.

The synergy was perfect: Helen led our efforts to bring love and resources to the teachers and children in the schools, and their parents deeply appreciated all they were doing for their kids. When Dr. Record opened Christ Health Center across the street, the women pointed teachers and parents to the clinic where they could get the finest of care for a fraction of the cost of other facilities. Between the clinic and the school was an old firehouse that was closing down. We saw it as a perfect place to serve kids breakfast

ALL OF THIS HAPPENED ONLY BECAUSE TWO PEOPLE WERE ALREADY PASSIONATE ABOUT HELPING PEOPLE AND WERE FULLY ENGAGED IN REACHING OUT TO A DISADVANTAGED COMMUNITY.

in the morning before school and provide classes and services for the entire community throughout the day.

All of this happened only because two people — Helen James and Robert Record — were already passionate about helping people and were fully engaged in reaching out to a disadvantaged community. Pastor Chris didn't create the ministry to teachers and students, and he didn't have the idea for the clinic. He just watched as God worked in the lives of two extraordinary individuals, and he offered to help with facilities, resources and leadership.

SCALE

AT OUR CHURCH

At our church in Baton Rouge, our first Stage 3 expression was a pickup truck and a trailer so we could deliver food to communities where poverty and hunger drained the life out of people. As we coordinated our efforts with a local ministry partner, we realized food stamps ran out in many homes near the end of the month . . . every month . . . and families were going hungry. A man who worked in one of these neighborhoods told me about the need, and he mentioned that he was growing vegetables on a plot of land in town. He picked his vegetables and gave bags of them to people he knew who could use some extra groceries. As soon as he told me what he was doing, I had to take a look. I drove down to his place, and

I walked into a virtual forest of vegetables.

He was actively involved in a Stage 2 outreach, and I wanted to help. We bought an old pickup and a trailer, and we looked for surplus food we could distribute. It was like Field of Dreams: if you create a system of distribution, the food will come. Before long, truckloads of all kinds of food drove up and parked in our lot. For years, this was one of the most effective outreach programs in our church. Do you think the people in those communities noticed? Of course, they did! Some of them wanted to come to a church that loved them enough to provide food for them when they were hungry. I suspect their response wasn't much different than the people on the hillside when Jesus fed the 5,000 and the 4,000. We didn't buy or build a clinic, a farm, or a nine-acre facility near Hollywood, but we had love, a truck and trailer, and newly opened eyes to look for resources to meet the needs of poor people. Every sustained serve, no matter what form it takes, is a dramatic statement to the entire community: the church is driving a stake in the ground that's not going anywhere.

I wanted everyone in our church to know they were a part of our ongoing, visible presence in the community. On many Sundays, I put pictures on the screen and told our people, "Look at how God has used us. God gave us 170 pallets of food to give away this month. Look at the expressions on these people's faces! They're thankful to God, and they're thankful to you." And I could often tell them, "This week as we delivered food, we had some incredible conversations with people. Three of them trusted in Christ! Isn't that fantastic? And it's all because God is using

EVERY SUSTAINED SERVE, NO MATTER WHAT FORM IT TAKES, IS A DRAMATIC STATEMENT TO THE ENTIRE COMMUNITY

you to care for those in need." The enthusiasm of our people caused them to look for more people to help and more resources to distribute. And they opened their wallets and purses to fund this effort. Together, we asked God to expand our reach, and we prayed that God would provide us with two more trucks, two more trailers, and a lot more semis full of groceries. Our hearts always asked, "How can we find more people to love? And how can we find more and better food to give them?"

One Sunday after I had shown how God was using our church to feed hungry people, a man came up to me and said, "I have a small, empty warehouse. I can't sell it, and I can't rent it. Can you use it as a place where you can sort food?" I was thrilled. It became our staging area where we could bring all the food, store what we weren't using that day, and distribute the rest to neighborhoods. We didn't start with a warehouse, and in fact, I didn't even know how important one would be. When we began using it, the warehouse made us much more efficient and effective. It became our missions outpost, and it enabled us to expand much more rapidly than before. The opportunity to use the warehouse didn't appear until we began delivering groceries from a truck and trailer. When we took the first small step, God showed up with the next big step.

A Stage 3 outreach can use a room at your church or a truck, or it can happen with no facilities at all. Jimmy and Irene Rollins, Lead Pastors of i5 Church in Glen Burnie, Maryland, have a passion to impact a generation of young people that are often forgotten. While noticing a need to keep students engaged after school and throughout the summer, the sports ministry, i5 Elite, was birthed. Since its inception, i5 Elite has grown from 20 kids learning about proper nutrition and physical fitness to a full-fledged youth track and field program. Currently with over 250 students that compete

> " A TURNING POINT IN STAGE 3 IS WHEN SOME OF THE PEOPLE IN THE COMMUNITY WHO HAVE RECEIVED CARE BECOME THE VOLUNTEERS, AND EVEN BECOME THE LEADERS OF THE OUTREACH MINISTRY. "

both locally and nationally, i5 Elite is making an impact on the track and in the lives of individuals and families. This program has changed the front door of the church. Many people who would have never entered the doors of a church have discovered purpose and have found community through track and field. What started out in Stage 1 was a personal passion for sports and the next generation. Stage 2 was an All Call with like-minded people and students with a need to be met. Stage 3 was a youth track and field program involving students, parents, coaches, and community leaders.

A turning point in Stage 3 is when some of the people in the community who have received care become the volunteers, and even become the leaders of the outreach ministry. They know the neighborhoods better than we do, and now they begin to own the ministry. They may begin by attending the church and then becoming volunteers to care for their own community. A few of them have leadership skills, so the ones who began the ministry gradually turn over the responsibility to these new leaders.

When your church has consistent connections in Stage 2 outreaches, be observant, and ask God to show you how and when some of these efforts might turn into permanent, daily, Stage 3 activities. As always, you'll look for leaders who have vision, heart, time, and skills, men and women who are proving themselves in Stage 2 activities. Churches might find they have a natural fit with a food pantry, clothing distribution, a soup kitchen,

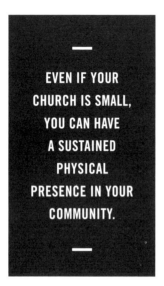

EVEN IF YOUR CHURCH IS SMALL, YOU CAN HAVE A SUSTAINED PHYSICAL PRESENCE IN YOUR COMMUNITY.

after-school activities and tutoring, cooking for the homeless, job training and placement, providing housing for an at-risk population, or other services. In many cases, people in the church or in the community find out that you're doing great work in Stage 2 outreaches, and they offer facilities so a regular Stage 2 outreach can become a sustained, identifiable Stage 3 ministry.

One of the first facilities we had in Baton Rouge was The Ascension House, a six-bed home and job training program for men experiencing homelessness. A man who owned a tiny church came to us and asked, "Do you want this building? I can't do anything with it, but maybe you can." Yes, we wanted it. We added another room so we could create space for six beds. The building was small, but it gave us a place to have a profound ministry. We had the bedrooms, a kitchen, a couple of bathrooms with a shower in the back, and a very small classroom. We put a fence around it to provide a sense of safety and security. The leaders taught and discipled the men. To pay for all the expenses, the men became part of a landscaping company the leader supervised. The Ascension House is still operating today. It has meant the world to the men who have come there.

STAGE 3 PRINCIPLES

STAGE 3 ACTIVITIES

Stage 3 activities almost always grow out of Stage 2 successes, and they are usually led by Stage 2 leaders. Even if your church is small, you can have a sustained physical presence in your community. If you don't have many resources, ask God to provide them. He'll probably send people, facilities and supplies from places you never dreamed existed. Here are some principles to guide you.

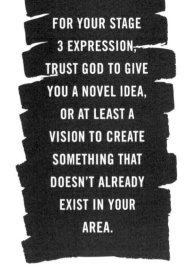

FOR YOUR STAGE 3 EXPRESSION, TRUST GOD TO GIVE YOU A NOVEL IDEA, OR AT LEAST A VISION TO CREATE SOMETHING THAT DOESN'T ALREADY EXIST IN YOUR AREA.

 (1) ***DON'T REINVENT THE WHEEL.***

In Stage 2, your church may partner with an organization like the YWCA (which has 250 beds for women at risk in our city), but don't try to duplicate an organization like that in a Stage 3 effort. Stick with the partnership, and devote as many people and resources as you can. If you try to create something like this on your own, you'll expend tremendous time, energy and money, the learning curve will be steep and long, and you probably won't do as good a job meeting needs as the existing organization.

For your Stage 3 expression, trust God to give you a novel idea, or at least a vision to create something that doesn't already exist in your area. Look at what other churches are doing in their communities, like the LA Dream Center, and learn from them. You might want to partner with them, send people on vision trips to see firsthand, and share resources. We want to create a network of support and prayer so many more churches will have a profound impact on their communities.

FROM THE BEGINNING OF STAGE 1, TREAT PEOPLE WITH DIGNITY, AND AVOID ANY HINT OF PATERNALISM.

Yes, we're doing good, but we need to avoid being do-gooders at all cost! Watch for verbiage that says "us and them," demeaning words and tones that make people Jesus loves feel small . . . feel like objects . . . and believe they are only projects for rich people. It's important to ask ourselves over and over again, "Who are the heroes in this story?" Jesus? Yes, certainly. Us? No, we need to understand we're only vessels channeling the grace of God into the lives of others. The people we care for? Yes, absolutely. They may be struggling with an addiction, their kids, work, finances, and finding a place to live, but their lives require enormous courage to take one more step. We take a lot of privileges and resources for granted; they can't take anything for granted. If they take even the first step to admit they need help, that's amazing bravery! In everything you do, shine the spotlight on Jesus and on the people who reach out to accept the love and resources we offer in His name.

For example, as I've mentioned, when we collect gifts for kids at Christmas, we don't give the presents to the children; we invite the parents to pick the gifts out and take them home to give them to their kids. We try to avoid

IN EVERYTHING YOU DO, SHINE THE SPOTLIGHT ON JESUS...

negative labels like "homeless." The Memphis Dream Center doesn't have a "homeless ministry"; they call it their Downtown Friends ministry. And at the LA Dream Center, the leaders teach volunteers to share their own names first when they meet people. We trust them with a part of ourselves before we ask them to trust us with part of their lives.

CREATE A SYSTEM THAT PERPETUATES THE RESOURCES.

Start with the end in mind. Don't rush to begin a grand plan without thinking through the systems, procedures, manpower, and resources you'll need for it to be a success . . . and don't overestimate all of your resources. Make sure they're real and committed. Compassionate people can afford to be spontaneous in Stage 1, but they need to have a plan in Stage 2. By Stage 3, leaders don't need an MBA from Harvard, but they need a sound, thoroughly vetted business plan that includes strengths, weaknesses, opportunities, and risks. They need to have their leadership established and their funding secured. A sustained serve must be led by people who have a robust blend of tenderness and toughness, a vision for the future and a clear-eyed look at today. A good start isn't enough. The plan needs to identify what's needed for the next three to five years . . . and maybe longer. Of course, there will be surprises and disappointments, so adjustments will be made, but shrewdness is an essential leadership component from the first thought of a Stage 3 presence.

 ## CREATE A LEADERSHIP PIPELINE.

One of the biggest strains on any new venture is caused by underestimating the work it takes to pull it off. When a church creates a culture of caring (see the next chapter), they expose people to needs and opportunities, their compassion deepens, and they get a clearer vision of how God can use them. In other words, Stage 1 SERVE Days get at least some people excited

> " ONE OF THE BIGGEST STRAINS ON ANY NEW VENTURE IS CAUSED BY UNDERESTIMATING THE WORK IT TAKES TO PULL IT OFF. "

about being involved in Stage 2 ongoing outreaches, and this involvement motivates at least some of them to become leaders or volunteers in Stage 3. But don't expect Stage 3 leaders to drop from the sky. They are the product of cutting-edge involvement and leadership development in the first two stages.

And let's be realistic: Some people who are enthusiastic to start may realize they've bitten off more than they can chew, so they drop out. If you don't have more people waiting in the wings to participate, you could be in big trouble by promising services your leadership structure can't deliver. Don't let that happen! Keep your attention focused on the whole pipeline so you can identify people with a growing blend of enthusiasm, skill, and commitment all along the way. Small groups are the natural incubators of leadership, enthusiasm, and service. As people support each other, they're less likely to burn out. And together, they pool their collective gifts, so there's less stress on any one person.

In our church, the pipeline has a simple and effective four-step growth track. The first is the essentials of the gospel and membership at the church, the second includes the basics of Christian growth, the third focuses on spiritual gifts and finding a place to serve in the body, and the fourth is placement on a serving team. These four are titled Know God, Find Freedom, Discover Purpose, and Make a Difference. This is our church's vision statement.

KNOW GOD >>>>> FIND FREEDOM >>>>> DISCOVER PURPOSE >>>>> MAKE A DIFFERENCE

The payoff of Stage 3 outreach is nothing less than community transformation. Our physical, persistent, loving presence changes the trajectory of the lives of individuals and their families, and over time, it affects the culture of the neighborhoods. When the love, grace, and power of God sinks into the pores of the city, broken families are reconciled, crime goes down, education levels go up, addicts get clean, hate is melted by love, racism is eroded by radical acceptance, and hopelessness is replaced by a new sense of hope. This deep, lasting change doesn't just

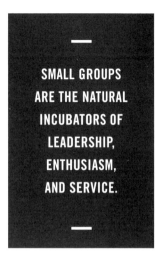

SMALL GROUPS ARE THE NATURAL INCUBATORS OF LEADERSHIP, ENTHUSIASM, AND SERVICE.

happen. We recognize another force wants to keep people locked in bondage to fear, hate, drugs, and shame. We're in a fight against Satan and evil, and we follow Jesus, our commander. We take Paul's admonition seriously:

> Finally, be strong in the Lord and in his mighty power. Put on the full armor of God, so that you can take your stand against the devil's schemes. For our struggle is not against flesh and blood, but against the rulers, against the authorities, against the powers of this dark world and against the spiritual forces of evil in the heavenly realms. Therefore put on the full armor of God, so that when the day of evil comes, you may be able to stand your ground, and after you have done everything, to stand. (Ephesians 6:10–13)

On the other side of the equation, the changes that occur in those who serve are just as profound and surprising—when Christians are involved in compassionate outreach to the poor and disadvantaged, God does something wonderful in their hearts, too. Our people have become wiser, stronger, more tender, more honest about their own struggles, and more dependent on the power of God to change lives. In fact, I believe true discipleship doesn't happen until and unless people become deeply involved in acts of compassion toward others—especially others who are very different from them. This involvement strips away our preconceptions, breaks down the walls that kept us safe, and erodes our judgmental attitudes toward those who are different from us. Serving those who can't repay us puts us more in touch with the heart of Jesus, who served people who can't possibly repay Him—people like you and me. Serving, then, is all about God's grace to us flowing into us, through us, and from us into the lives of others . . . with no strings attached.

Helen James knows something about recruiting leaders for the cause. As the concept of a sustained serve in Birmingham was beginning to take shape for her and Dr. Record, she saw that Dave Anderson's heart fit perfectly with the vision. Dave, his wife, and their four daughters lived in another part of Birmingham, and Dave had a "small group" of 40 boys. When Helen told him about their plans for the health clinic and schools, Dave instantly saw the amazing potential. He responded, "Why wouldn't we go there and be part of that?"

Dave and his family moved into a house near the clinic—a house that was across the street from Section 8 government housing. He moved his group of boys to the new location in the disadvantaged part of town because he believed God wanted him to have an impact on many more kids.

> **WHEN CHRISTIANS ARE INVOLVED IN COMPASSIONATE OUTREACH TO THE POOR AND DISADVANTAGED, GOD DOES SOMETHING WONDERFUL IN THEIR HEARTS, TOO.**

> **THIS IS WHERE GOD HAS CALLED US TO BE, AND THIS IS WHAT GOD HAS CALLED US TO DO.**

Very quickly, Dave's love for children became evident to the families across the street, but his involvement with them wasn't without plenty of drama. After only a couple of months, a mother who lived with her brother and her four young sons stabbed her brother. Someone called Dave, and he got there as the man lay in a pool of blood on the floor. He picked up the four boys and carried them out of the apartment as the police came to arrest their mom.

The story doesn't end there. Ten years later, as Dave and some boys played ball in a yard, the ball rolled away and was picked up by a young man. It was one of the boys he had carried over their uncle's blood years before. Dave realized this wasn't a chance event: God had brought this boy, now a young man, back into his life so he could share the love of God with him.

Dave is the dad, the teacher, the big brother, and the role model all these young men desperately need. His ministry philosophy is simple: "I treat them like I'd treat my own sons." Living across from government housing carries a degree of risk for Dave and his family. They hear fights and gunshots, and there have been nearby murders. Over the 25 years they've lived in the neighborhood, there have been some moments when Dave wondered if he needed to move his family to a safer part of the city, but he has resisted the urge. He insists, "This is where God has called us to be, and this is what God has called us to do."

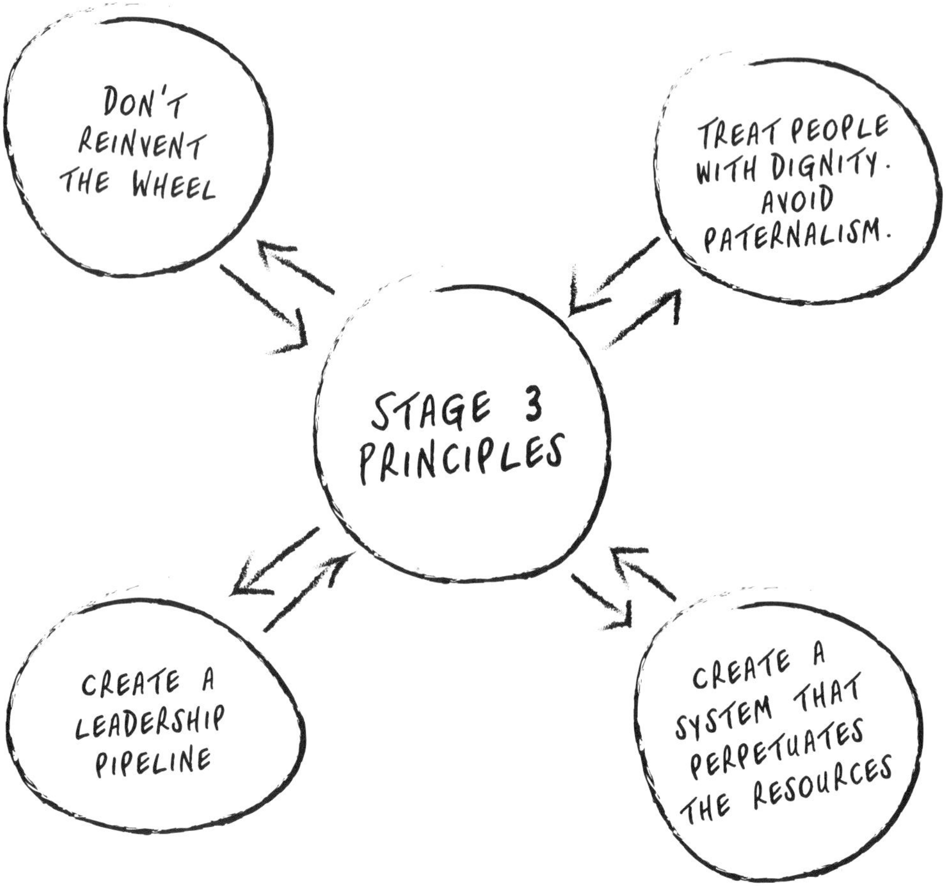

DON'T REINVENT THE WHEEL

TREAT PEOPLE WITH DIGNITY. AVOID PATERNALISM.

STAGE 3 PRINCIPLES

CREATE A LEADERSHIP PIPELINE

CREATE A SYSTEM THAT PERPETUATES THE RESOURCES

Our work in the schools, our purchasing and running Christ Health Center, and our mentoring of young people at the firehouse aren't just to relieve a moment of despair from time to time. Our goal is to see God transform lives, to bring His light into the darkness, and to radically change the neighborhood so God's mercy, truth, and justice reign.

The establishment of a Stage 3 sustained serve is the product of a long process of Stage 1 All Call involvement of everyone in the church (everyone who chooses to participate, that is) and the establishment of consistent connections in various forms in Stage 2. A sustained serve may be as mobile as a truck and trailer or as small as a room in a church or a home. But getting it started is only the first step in Stage 3. Gifted, godly leaders trust God to see the ministry deepen, sharpen, and expand to meet more needs, provide more services, and connect to more resources. Like all of us in our spiritual journeys, leaders in Stage 3 are always dependent, always on the cutting edge, and always growing and maturing.

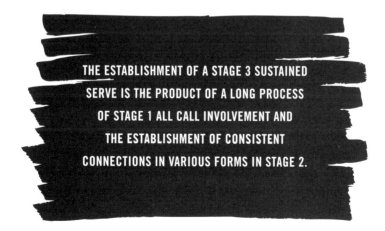

THE ESTABLISHMENT OF A STAGE 3 SUSTAINED SERVE IS THE PRODUCT OF A LONG PROCESS OF STAGE 1 ALL CALL INVOLVEMENT AND THE ESTABLISHMENT OF CONSISTENT CONNECTIONS IN VARIOUS FORMS IN STAGE 2.

LUKE 14:12–14

Then Jesus said to his host, "When you give a luncheon or dinner, do not invite your friends, your brothers or sisters, your relatives, or your rich neighbors; if you do, they may invite you back and so you will be repaid. But when you give a banquet, invite the poor, the crippled, the lame, the blind, and you will be blessed. Although they cannot repay you, you will be repaid at the resurrection of the righteous."

1

Has this chapter challenged and reframed your concept of a Stage 3 sustained serve in your community? Explain your answer.

....
....
....
....
....
....
....

THINK ABOUT IT

2

How can leaders tell when a Stage 2 involvement is ready to become a sustained serve?

....
....
....
....
....
....
....

3

How would you define paternalism? How does it poison relationships with people who are treated as "less than"? How will you help your people treat others with dignity and respect?

....
....
....
....
....
....
....
....
....
....

....
....

4

How is your leadership pipeline working? How can it be improved?

....
....
....
....
....
....
....
....
....

5

Is the idea of having a sustained serve in your community thrilling or threatening to you? Explain your answer.

....

....

....

....

....

....

....

....

....

....

....

....

....

....

....

....

....

....

....

The load, or weight, or burden of my neighbor's glory should be laid daily on my back, a load so heavy that only humility can carry it, and the backs of the proud will be broken. . . . This does not mean that we are to be perpetually solemn. We must play. But our merriment must be of that kind (and it is, in fact, the merriest kind) which exists between people who have, from the outset, taken each other seriously—no flippancy, no superiority, no presumption. And our charity must be a real and costly love, with deep feeling for the sins in spite of which we love the sinner—no mere tolerance or indulgence which parodies love as flippancy parodies merriment.

C.S. LEWIS
The Weight of Glory

CHAPTER SIX

NEXT STEPS

OVER THE YEARS

Over the years as I've led outreach ministries, I've made a lot of mistakes, but probably the biggest one is the failure to consistently and persuasively communicate that every believer can make a difference in the lives of those in need. As I've mentioned, ten percent of the people in our churches have a God-given thirst to pour themselves out to care for the poor, widows, orphans, immigrants, the disabled, single moms, the elderly, addicts, and others in desperate need. It's easy to inspire them; they're a pool of gas waiting for a match! It's the other ninety percent who need the Spirit of God to get under their skin and change their perceptions and motivations. They live in a chasm between the real needs in the community and their less-than-passionate motivation to meet those needs. Our job is to narrow that chasm.

We've worked really hard to make SERVE Days as easy and positive as possible for our people, but still, only half of our people show up. This tells me we may not be putting the outreach cookies on the bottom shelf. Certainly, we don't expect All Calls to literally involve all the people in the church, but our goal is to attract, inspire, and involve more than half. All of us have to

OUR GOAL IS TO ATTRACT, INSPIRE, AND INVOLVE...

find the balance between leaning in too hard to talk about our responsibility before God to care for the lost and the least . . . and not leaning in hard enough, leaving our people self-absorbed, uninformed, and uninspired about the needs outside the walls of the church. Sometimes I can be loud and passionate—maybe a little too loud and passionate—and I may come across too strong for some people. But I certainly don't want to pull back too much and appear to be uncaring and uncommitted. Helping me find this balance is one of the responsibilities of our outreach team.

Whether you're just starting an outreach ministry or you're well on the way into Stages 2 (consistent connections) and 3 (a sustained serve), let me offer some next steps for you to consider.

 CREATE EFFECTIVE ON-RAMPS.

Stage 1 is the All Call, and discovery is at the heart of this stage. In the preparation for these events, you'll uncover needs in the community you may not have known about before, and at the events, your people will get "up close and personal" with people who aren't normally on their radars.

SERVE Days are the biggest and best pathways for the most people to get involved in outreach, but even there, think about the activities that provide the biggest bang for your people. Make the breakfast special, provide outstanding leaders for each event (and for church plants and small churches, that outstanding leader is probably you!), give them all the resources they'll need, bring them back together to have lunch and share their stories, and celebrate like crazy the next day in church. These activities are short-term, low risk, high touch, family friendly, and lots of fun. In other words, by Sunday morning, people who didn't go should be kicking themselves for missing such a great event!

THE BEST ON-RAMPS FOR MANY CHURCHES ARE THE POWERFUL LINKS BETWEEN SMALL GROUPS AND LOCAL NONPROFIT ORGANIZATIONS

As the ministry develops into Stage 2, the best on-ramps for many churches are the powerful links between small groups and local nonprofit organizations, schools, nursing homes, and other facilities. Just as the process never ends of finding new and effective activities for SERVE Days, stay on the hunt for new opportunities to connect new small groups with organizations, or perhaps, groups that have existed for a while but are now ready to make a Stage 2 commitment to a partnership.

A sustained serve is well established with people, places, and resources, but even there, some people may volunteer temporarily as their first venture into compassion ministries. Even a church's Stage 3 ministry can be an on-ramp for them.

Pray, think, and look for the progression through Stages 1 and 2. Sooner or later, as God opens doors, these leaders will find a way to have this permanent, powerful presence in their cities. Each one may look very different, from a truck and trailer to a nine-acre campus with incredible facilities. Look around, visit some, and let God move you to do great things in your city.

UNCOVER AND RESOURCE CREATIVE IDEAS FOR OUTREACH.

As this ministry develops, you can count on people coming up with a ton of ideas about how the church can reach an overlooked segment of the community. Many of these are terrific ideas. Encourage the people who come up with good ideas, and provide resources to help them express the love of Christ in their world. Be diplomatic with the people whose ideas don't pass muster. Affirm their hearts and creativity, and point them to be involved in ministries that are close to their new passion.

CARE FOR THE UP-AND-COMERS AS WELL AS THE DOWN-AND-OUTERS.

People who are successful in business or professions may not be as successful in their personal lives. They may be just as distraught as poor people about strains with their spouse and kids, their financial problems, and substance abuse, but they hide their pain behind the walls of nice houses, inside their luxury cars, and under fine clothes. As you consistently share your heart for hurting people, you'll probably find that some people in your church have a heart to break through the façade of those who aren't poor. Behind the masks, they'll uncover deep hurts and heal gaping wounds. These compassionate people know how to open doors and how to provide comfort and care to those who have tried so hard to keep their pain a secret.

> **" AFFIRM THEIR HEARTS AND CREATIVITY, AND POINT THEM TO BE INVOLVED IN MINISTRIES THAT ARE CLOSE TO THEIR NEW PASSION. "**

> **CELEBRATE THEIR DESIRE TO PROVIDE RESOURCES SO THE MINISTRY CAN BE EFFECTIVE AND EXPAND.**

We may also find that some wealthy people want to be involved with the church's outreach ministry, but they'd rather give generously or make connections with leaders of nonprofits than work in a soup kitchen or roll up their sleeves and clean up a playground. And some of these men and women are so busy running their companies that they don't have time to spend in outreach activities. Don't condemn them for being absent on SERVE Days. Instead, celebrate their desire to provide resources so the ministry can be effective and expand.

4. ENLIST A DIGITAL TEAM.

We invite everybody to be involved in All Calls, but some people aren't in a place to be involved in Stage 2 partnerships. They may be single moms who can't leave their kids, or they may be disabled and unable to travel very easily. We've found that some of these people can channel their passion digitally to connect with people. Some people on our digital team have served the poor and motivated our people by keeping our social media fresh and alive. That's a vital contribution to the cause! And realize this: a lot of people we serve have technology that enables them to connect with us—and after they connect, we read their posts, listen to their calls, and know their hearts.

COMMUNICATE IN A WAY THAT PROVIDES UPDATED INFORMATION, COMPELLING STORIES, AND CONTINUOUS PERSONAL CONNECTIONS.

Evaluate your social media presence, and make it a conversation. Don't just post, but listen, read, like, and comment when others are posting about serving. Communicate in a way that provides updated information, compelling stories, and continuous personal connections. Today, people expect to be able to participate in their own way on their own time. We can offer a range of serving opportunities online for individuals or groups, and they can click on the one they want to tackle. They may look at it when they're awake at 2:00 in the morning, and they do the task at lunch the next day. We can offer several possibilities, so if one is taken, several more are available. And each one has all the information anyone needs to make it happen. The is the "Uber approach" to personalized, instant access outreach, and it's the wave of the future.

That's the future of outreach, but the present is to put all the information and sign-ups for our SERVE Days online so people can do everything on their mobile phones. That's not tomorrow; that's today.

 CREATE A COLLABORATIVE SERVICE ECONOMY.

When we crack the code of the needs in our communities, we discover the problems are far too big, encompassing, and difficult than we ever imagined. Every single need connects to a host of other problems like a spider web of heartache. Alone, our efforts are just a drop in the bucket, so we need to leverage our time, talents, and resources in partnerships with outstanding organizations in our communities. If we insist on remaining a silo, we won't see our community as a whole, and we won't develop powerful relationships to provide more resources for people in need. For instance, one of our partners provides warehouse space, another provides food and materials, and we provide the manpower to organize and distribute it. The other organizations have donors, and we give to the cause, too. Together, we accomplish far more for the kingdom of God than if each of us worked in isolation.

TOGETHER, WE ACCOMPLISH FAR MORE FOR THE KINGDOM OF GOD THAN IF EACH OF US WORKED IN ISOLATION.

When Hurricane Harvey hit South Texas, over 20 ARC pastors and local churches banded together as brothers in extraordinary ways. Churches from near and far marshalled resources and manpower, working together to serve the community. I told these pastors that if we can lay down our logos and egos and come together to care for the city, we can make a major impact for God's kingdom. And that's exactly what happened. Over the next hours, days, and weeks, these pastors worked as an eager, tireless team, exchanging resources, sharing storage space, enlisting volunteer support, meeting each other's needs, swapping advice, and encouraging one another in prayer and love. Pastor Scott Jones of Grace Church in Humble, Texas, said the text thread among us "was going off like the 4th of July!" It was beautiful!

Everyone freely helped one another—it was a true Book of Acts community. Today, these pastors remain in relationship, encouraging one another and working together to change their city. Dream Centers have been birthed, church culture has been changed, influence with the city has been made, and the body of Christ has been unified.

WE WANT TO USE OUR PORTION OF THE TEN PERCENT IN WAYS THAT MAGNIFY OUR IMPACT IN CARING FOR THE POOR.

6 ALLOCATE MONEY FOR OUTREACH.

Effective outreach ministries don't just happen. They need dollars to make them go. This is a topic I talk to pastors about all the time. Let me explain my suggestion: Most churches give ten percent of their income to missions; that's standard. Of that ten percent, you can divide it into several categories: international missions, national outreaches, and local outreach ministries—including everything we've been talking about in this book. I recommend allocating about 30 percent of a church's missions budget to local outreach activities: SERVE Day, partnerships with food pantries, toys the police department gives away at Christmas, the church's Stage 3 sustained serve, and all the rest. Remember that many of the small groups are self-funding their work with partnerships, but some groups will need a bit of a financial boost to make the partnerships work most effectively. The partner organizations sometimes provide matching funds, so look for those opportunities to leverage your contributions.

We want to use our portion of the ten percent in ways that magnify our impact in caring for the poor. The needs are too great and the cause is too important for us to waste any money, time, or passion. We need to maximize every resource. In this way, the kingdom of God expands exponentially.

7 INFORM AND MOTIVATE YOUR PEOPLE.

I recommend you get a copy of this book for every leader in your church so they understand the philosophy, strategy, and process of creating an effective outreach ministry. I'd also get copies of Servolution for every person in your congregation. The stories and principles in this book will inspire them to get involved in SERVE Days, partnerships, and perhaps, even A sustained serve in the community. (100% of the profits from the sale of the books go back to a non-profit ministry to be used for additional outreach and training.)

At the end of this book, you'll find links to a wealth of resources you can use to help you launch and develop all three stages of this ministry. It's all free, so use them, adapt them, and let them spur you to create your own. Dream big, pray in faith, and watch what God will do.

✔ NEXT STEPS TO-DO:

- ☐ CREATE EFFECTIVE ON-RAMPS.

- ☐ UNCOVER AND RESOURCE CREATIVE IDEAS FOR OUTREACH.

- ☐ CARE FOR THE UP-AND-COMERS AS WELL AS THE DOWN-AND-OUTERS.

- ☐ ENLIST A DIGITAL TEAM.

- ☐ CREATE A COLLABORATIVE SERVICE ECONOMY.

- ☐ ALLOCATE MONEY FOR OUTREACH.

- ☐ INFORM AND MOTIVATE YOUR PEOPLE.

EPHESIANS 5:1-2

Follow God's example, therefore, as dearly loved children and walk in the way of love, just as Christ loved us and gave himself up for us as a fragrant offering and sacrifice to God.

1

What does it mean to "lean in too hard" and "not lean in hard enough" in our communication about outreach in our communities?

....
....
....
....
....
....
....

2

How can you make your on-ramps more attractive and meaningful?

....
....
....
....
....
....
....

THINK ABOUT IT

3

How can you develop an effective digital team? What are the goals, what might be the benefits, and what are some stages of progress you envision?

....
....
....
....
....
....
....
....
....
....

4

How would you define and describe a "collaborative service economy"?

....
....
....
....
....
....
....
....
....
....

5

What is your outreach
budget? What does it
need to be?

....
....
....
....
....
....
....
....
....
....

6

Take some time to write
your plans for the next
steps in your outreach
ministry.

....
....
....
....
....
....
....
....
....

We sometimes think of compassion as "kind intention." The Gospel writers meant more than that. The word actually means, "to have trembling bowels." In other words, biblical compassion is such a deep degree of care that it gnaws at your gut.

BEN DAILEY
Collide

CHAPTER SEVEN

BEATING COMPASSION FATIGUE

I *THOUGHT WE WERE READY.*

I thought we were ready. We weren't. *WE WEREN'T.*

Everybody near the coast of Louisiana kept an eye on the news during the last week of August in 2005. The radar showed a strengthening hurricane in the Gulf, and it was headed for the mouth of the Mississippi. Those who have lived long enough in that part of the country know they should take these forecasts with a grain of salt. Seldom do storms hit where the predictions forecast . . . especially several days out.

Still, we knew it was going to be big no matter where it made landfall. As soon as the National Weather Service confirmed it was on the way, we started our preparations. We sent emails to our volunteers to fill them in on the plans and make sure they knew when and where to show up when the time came. We contacted the mayor's office and other city officials to offer our assistance and coordinate efforts, and I called the leader of our cooking team. I asked him to order food for seven or eight thousand people, but I also cautioned him not to buy too much food because if we didn't use it, it would spoil. By this time, we had a network of pastors whose churches

WE HAD A NETWORK OF PASTORS WHOSE CHURCHES WERE COMMITTED TO WORK TOGETHER TO HELP WHEREVER THE NEED MAY BE.

were committed to work together to help wherever the need may be.

As the days passed, the National Weather Service predicted the storm, named Katrina, was still headed for the Louisiana coast, and it had strengthened to a Category 5 storm! A few days before landfall, voluntary and mandatory evacuations were ordered, so people were already streaming up the highway out of New Orleans to Baton Rouge. The storm was to hit early in the morning on August 29. Again, I made dozens of calls to be sure we were ready.

That morning, the news reported that the storm surge, the wind, and the rain were significant, but New Orleans had dodged a bullet. The damage didn't appear too bad. But a few minutes later, my friend Steve Robinson, pastor of Mandeville Church of the King, called me. He sounded frantic: "I just heard that the levees broke and New Orleans is flooding."

I assured him we'd been through floods before and we'd make it through this one. But he insisted, "No, Dino, you don't understand. This is massive flooding. The levees have been breached in many areas and the city is in chaos. The 9th Ward is under 12 feet of water, and downtown New Orleans is almost completely covered!"

I turned on the television, and I was shocked by what I saw. Water was everywhere, up to the roofs of houses, and rushing through the huge breaks in the levees. People were breaking holes in their roofs to climb out and signal for help, and dead animals were floating in the streets.

From that moment for the foreseeable future, I had one task: to rescue as many people and provide as much relief as possible. It was thrilling, consuming, and inspiring. Pastors and their churches from all over the area, and soon the entire country, came to South Louisiana to help. More than 450 of us had already formed the Pastors Resource Council, and we all got to work. I became the air traffic controller to steer people and resources where they were desperately needed—which was just about everywhere! And I coordinated with all these pastors to be sure their churches felt valued and their people had plenty of materials, food, clothing, and other resources.

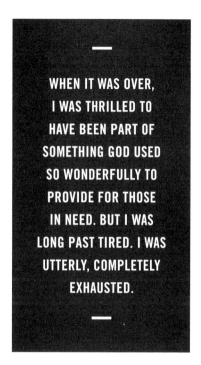

WHEN IT WAS OVER, I WAS THRILLED TO HAVE BEEN PART OF SOMETHING GOD USED SO WONDERFULLY TO PROVIDE FOR THOSE IN NEED. BUT I WAS LONG PAST TIRED. I WAS UTTERLY, COMPLETELY EXHAUSTED.

For 200 days, we gave it all we had. We worked with 500 faith-based organizations, assisted 684 counselors and chaplains to care for spiritual and emotional needs, used 1,587 delivery trucks, scheduled 5,952 medical visits, enlisted 14,092 volunteers, served 2,853,100 people, and distributed 61,260,000 pounds of food, clothes, and other resources.[1]

When it was over, I was thrilled to have been part of something God used so wonderfully to provide for those in need. It's what our church was all about. But I was long past tired. I was utterly, completely exhausted.

---

1   For more on this story, read Chapter 5, "Hurricane Katrina: The Day the Levees Broke," in *Servolution*.

RUNNING ON EMPTY ▬▬▬

IT'S DRAINING TO LIVE UNDER THE PRESSURE

It's draining to live under the pressure of running programs, but leaders in business and the church do it all day every day. When we add the stresses and uncertainties of being integrally involved in the lives of the poor, our inner resources can be drained even more. Where do we find a deep well of inner strength so our hearts stay full and overflowing?

Many years ago, a pastor named B.B. Warfield studied the life of Christ and wrote an article called "The Emotional Life of Our Lord." In his study of the Gospels, he discovered that the writers described Jesus' compassion more than all other emotions combined. In fact, the Greek word translated as "compassion" actually means "His bowels trembled." Jesus experienced an "internal movement of pity" which led to "an external act of beneficence."[2] The translators use several terms to describe the compassion of Jesus. For instance, when Jesus and the disciples traveled through the community of Nain, a widow was about to bury her only son. Luke tells us Jesus' "heart went out to her" (Luke 7:13). When Jesus saw the thousands of people who had come to hear Him, "he had compassion on them, because they were like sheep without a shepherd." And after He noticed they had nothing to eat, He fed them all with a boy's sack lunch (Mark 6:34–44).

One of the most poignant moments in the Gospels occurred outside the tomb of His friend Lazarus, who had been dead four days. The man's sisters were disappointed Jesus hadn't come to heal their brother when he was sick. In response to the sisters, especially the tenderhearted Mary, and

---

2 "The Emotional Life of our Lord," B.B. Warfield, https://www.monergism.com/thethreshold/articles/onsite/emotionallife.html

the weeping of all the people there, Jesus "was deeply moved in spirit and troubled," and He raised Lazarus from the grave (John 11:33–44).

Jesus let His heart be broken by the desperate needs of people around Him. He wasn't primarily an administrator; He was a lover, a shepherd, a dear friend who was willing to absorb the hurt of others, and He let that hurt propel Him to action. Of course, the supreme act spurred by His compassion was His willingness to give himself completely and ultimately on the cross. Though Jesus argued with His critics and defended himself against the attacks of the self-righteous, in His relationships to the sick, the poor, foreigners, and people with any needs, we don't see Him guarding himself. Emotionally, physically, and spiritually, Jesus' love for them caused Him to identify fully with them and their plight. He was, as we say today, "all in."

But as we look at the life of Jesus through the eyes of the Gospel writers, we never see Him frantic, hurried, or frustrated. What gave Him such stability and wisdom? His was surely the most pressurized life ever lived! How could He cope with the enormous weight of responsibility? He found ways to regularly recharge His engines. He carved out long times of prayer so His relationship with the Father remained fresh and strong, He went on retreats with His closest followers, and they spent many hours walking from place to place. We can imagine they had many wonderful conversations on those walks. Times of prayer, relaxation, and reflection were crucial to Jesus, and they are crucial

> "
> **WHEN WE ADD THE STRESSES AND UNCERTAINTIES OF BEING INTEGRALLY INVOLVED IN THE LIVES OF THE POOR, OUR INNER RESOURCES CAN BE DRAINED EVEN MORE.**
> "

to us. We need to find sources of "renewable energy" as we lead our churches. If we don't, we run the risk of burning out . . . which is always ugly and painful, and it takes a long time to recuperate.

Jesus didn't go to every town and meet every need, and we can't either. He didn't have email and social media, but we do. Studies show that today, many of us are so wedded to our devices that we subconsciously are always ready to respond. Linda Stone, formerly an executive with Apple and Microsoft, described the constant distractions as "continuous partial attention." She writes:

> To pay continuous partial attention is to pay partial attention— CONTINUOUSLY. It is motivated by a desire to be a LIVE node on the network. Another way of saying this is that we want to connect and be connected. We want to effectively scan for opportunity and optimize for the best opportunities, activities, and contacts, in any given moment. To be busy, to be connected, is to be alive, to be recognized, and to matter. We pay continuous partial attention in an effort NOT TO MISS ANYTHING. It is an always-on, anywhere, anytime, anyplace behavior that involves an artificial sense of constant crisis. We are always in high alert when we pay continuous partial attention. This artificial sense of constant crisis is more typical of continuous partial attention than it is of multi-tasking. [3]

Through all kinds of media, phone, and online connections, we find out about far more needs than we can meet. We have to set realistic goals and limitations so we don't deplete our energy and erode our love. The first

---

3   Linda Stone. "Continuous Partial Attention," cited at
     lindastone.net/qa/continuous-partial-attention/

sign this is happening is that we become annoyed by people's needs, and the second sign is that we become cynical about those who cry out for help, about our people, and about our own motives for being involved. We've heard it all before, and we start believing it:

> WE HAVE TO SET REALISTIC GOALS AND LIMITATIONS SO WE DON'T DEPLETE OUR ENERGY AND ERODE OUR LOVE.

"The homeless want to live on the streets."

"Poor people are just irresponsible."

"They deserve the pain they're in."

"We should focus on the deserving poor."

"It won't make any difference. They'll be just as needy tomorrow."

"They're taking what we give them and they're selling it down the street."

"That person came back for a second bag of groceries. How selfish!"

CLARIFY YOUR LIMITS

WHEN OUR JOY OF CARING

When our joy of caring for people is vanishing, we need a fresh shot of God's love and grace. And many times, we just need to take a break and chill out for a while. In outreach ministries, we're managing the constant tension between unmet needs screaming for attention and our limited resources to meet those needs. Don't even try all this on your own! You need a team of mature, wise, competent people to help you. Outreach leadership teams aren't where you put people who have mediocre leadership skills. It's where you put your best people because this ministry demands more than almost any other. I've heard well-meaning pastors try to go it alone in coordinating their church's outreach ministry. One told me, "That's okay. I can do it. I'm drawing from the well of the love I have for people." I hated to tell him that his well almost certainly wasn't deep enough for the long haul. It would run dry sooner or later.

It's okay to say, "I'm sorry, but I can't help with that." As Jesus said, the poor will always be with us. Their needs will be there tomorrow, just as they are today. We won't do anybody any good if we crash and burn.

Yes, the needs in the community are deep and wide, but we can't rebuild the city by ourselves or in a short time. Our job each day is to put another brick on the wall. That's all, and that's enough. Do it with joy and love, and you'll have the strength to put another brick on the wall tomorrow.

One of the most important questions we need to ask, no matter what ministry we're leading, is simple and profound: Who deserves the credit? Do we want the acclaim, or are we pointing to Jesus? Are we truly serving Him, or are we really trying to advance our own agendas? (Don't answer these questions too quickly.)

OUR JOB EACH DAY IS TO PUT ANOTHER BRICK ON THE WALL. THAT'S ALL, AND THAT'S ENOUGH.

I know pastors who have moved into disaster areas who have given everything they've got for weeks and even months. They're utterly exhausted. They look awful and they sound awful, but they don't believe they can ever say, "I need a break." You can run like crazy for a few days, but our bodies (even young, strong bodies) need time to recover from excessive strains.

Are we too busy to pray, to meditate, to laugh, and to cry? Do our families feel neglected while we pour ourselves into the lives of people we don't really know? What are the spiritual disciplines that are fueling our souls? Who are the friends who are telling us the truth and encouraging us to create margin in our lives?

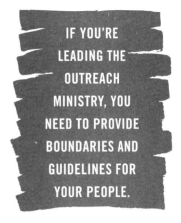

IF YOU'RE LEADING THE OUTREACH MINISTRY, YOU NEED TO PROVIDE BOUNDARIES AND GUIDELINES FOR YOUR PEOPLE.

Are we (and are our compassionate people) so busy that we become isolated from the broader faith community? Is our vision for social justice, caring for the poor, and righting society's wrongs keeping us connected to church and small groups, the sources of inspiration and encouragement, or has our vision become a compulsion that is eating us alive and creating resentment toward those who "aren't as committed"? We need to stay connected for many reasons: perspective, sanity, encouragement, correction, and a prayer covering, to name a few of the most important. If you're leading the outreach ministry, you need to provide boundaries and guidelines for your people. Who is providing those boundaries and limits for you? As I've mentioned, a strong small-group strategy for community engagement shares the burdens and multiplies the joys of serving. It doesn't solve everything, but it helps a lot.

Stage 1 activities have very clear boundaries: on SERVE Days, we're engaged in specific activities for a few hours, and we're done. In Stage 2, small groups often partner with nonprofits in the community, and people in these groups are often all over the board in their understanding of boundaries. A few people are reluctant participants; they're looking for any opportunity to pull out. But some tenderhearted men and women become too absorbed in meeting the needs of people. They need help in setting limits to their

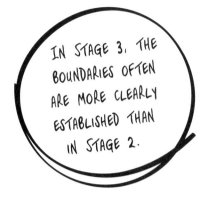

IN STAGE 3, THE BOUNDARIES OFTEN ARE MORE CLEARLY ESTABLISHED THAN IN STAGE 2.

involvement. In Stage 3, those involved generally are more tested and proven, and some are professional caregivers who have had to learn their boundaries over many years of interacting with people in need. In Stage 3, the boundaries often are more clearly established than in Stage 2.

The reason I love outreach is that I've learned to test the fences in any activity and partnership. I may have been clueless in the earliest days when we would do anything for anybody, but no longer. God has given me the wisdom of experience . . . which has come from plenty of failures, which is how most of us learn anything anyway. In Stage 2 and Stage 3, quite often the people who are most effective are the ones who have suffered the same heartaches as the ones they're serving. They're raw and real, which makes them wonderfully compassionate, but it also may easily cause them to go too far too fast, not even notice boundaries, and perhaps argue with their team leader when the leader tells them to slow down.

STAYING WISE, STRONG, AND FULL

I'VE LEARNED THE HARD WAY

I've learned the hard way over the years about the need for those who care to care for themselves, and especially, for leaders of outreach ministries to set clear boundaries for the people who serve with them. Here are some of the most important principles.

BE AWARE OF THE TENSION.

Anything that captures our hearts has the potential to drain us. Vision, passion, and dedication are wonderful traits in any leader or servant, but those who minister to the most disadvantaged in the community run the risk of losing perspective. I know because it's happened to me.

When the needs of people begin to consume us, we gradually make excuses about not spending time in prayer, reading the Scriptures, enjoying hobbies, and loving our families. In fact, before long, we feel guilty for doing any of these life-giving things! At some point, we begin to operate in our own strength, and soon we develop a grudge against people who don't seem to care as much or give as much as we do.

The tension between being "all in" and taking care of ourselves is very real. Acknowledge it, accept it, and create habits that keep you drinking deeply from the well of God's love, wisdom, and power.

> **THE TENSION BETWEEN BEING "ALL IN" AND TAKING CARE OF OURSELVES IS VERY REAL.**

 ### SURROUND YOURSELF WITH FRIENDS WHO SPEAK TRUTH TO YOU.

All of us, no matter our calling or level of leadership, need at least one or two wise, honest friends who have the courage to speak into our lives. Isolation inevitably leads to dumb decisions and disasters. You may not want to hear what your friends have to say, but listen. You'll be far more effective if you do.

WATCH FOR SIGNS OF BURNOUT.

At one point in Baton Rouge we were deeply involved in food distribution to the poor neighborhoods. In one week, we gave away 120,000 pounds of food. Three 18-wheelers showed up in our parking lot with a total of 88 pallets of groceries. I was excited that God had provided such a blessing, and I was determined to get it all out to hungry people, especially people who didn't look like us, talk like us, or believe like us. I believed God had given me a mandate to reach people who wouldn't normally show up at our church, but by this time, my passion wasn't tapping into God's love and strength. Soon, I was utterly exhausted and angry at those who weren't as dedicated as me.

My father-in-law pulled me aside near the end of that week and said, "Dino, you don't have to save the world. Jesus died for people, but He hasn't asked you to work yourself to death for them." He used the creation story to reorient my thinking. He said, "You need to be eating from the tree of life, not the other tree." His point was clear. I was trying to be a savior, but that wasn't my job description.

I had let the needs of people consume me. Every day, a car wreck, a dreaded diagnosis, a pink slip at work, or some other tragedy devastated individuals and families, and each one broke my heart. I realized I couldn't be there for everybody, but by the grace of God, I could be there for a few . . . and still be sane, strong, and happy, but only if I kept drinking from the source of living water.

I know I'm approaching burnout when I become cynical. When that poisonous perspective fills my heart, I don't trust the people around me, the people I serve, God, or myself. I become angry over almost anything, and I'm filled with the twin evils of pride and self-pity—pride that I'm so noble because I'm giving everything to help people . . . and self-pity that no one notices all I'm doing for others. (I know this is hard to read, but for some of us, it sounds too familiar.)

> **I WAS TRYING TO BE A SAVIOR, BUT THAT WASN'T MY JOB DESCRIPTION.**

The problem of burnout isn't just for you and me; it's for everyone involved in caring ministries. In a crisis, people can get close to the edge in a hurry! After Hurricane Katrina, we set up a kitchen. One morning about 2,000 people were lined up to get donuts someone had donated. I was inside while our people were handing out the donuts when some of them rushed in and told me, "Pastor, you need to come outside. We've got a problem!"

I'd been up all night, and I was exhausted. When I walked out the door, I had no idea what the problem might be. There was obviously a confrontation going on. The man on our team who was responsible to keep the line moving was screaming at people, "You're taking too many donuts! You can only have two!"

You need to know this: that man is one of the nicest, kindest people I know, but in the stress of that moment, he had flipped. I was witnessing a full-blown manic episode! I pulled him aside and said gently, "You need to go home." He tried to resist and insist on staying, but I said, "No, it's time for you to go home. We'll take it from here."

By this time, he was crying uncontrollably. Through his tears, he said, "But what about the inventory?"

"The inventory of donuts doesn't matter," I explained. "If giving out too many donuts wrecks the church, so be it, but we're still going to love these people and give them donuts. If they take more than two, it's probably because they're hungry or they're afraid they won't get another meal for a while. These people's lives have just been turned upside down. If they want three donuts, we're going to give them three donuts. Don't worry about the inventory. If we run out, I can go buy more, but if we treat them with disrespect, it'll be hard to repair the damage."

I realized at that moment that everybody can be involved in a relaxed All Call, but not everybody is wired to be face to face with desperate people during a disaster, walk with people through their deepest grief, help relapsing addicts, or deal patiently with angry and demanding people. This man should have been in the back room handling inventory at the warehouse or keeping the books, not in the front, interacting with people who were devastated and scared to death.

All of us have important roles to play, and all of us need to use our gifts by the power of the Holy Spirit to have an impact on needy and hurting people. However, as we see in the Scriptures, we have different gifts, as well as different experiences. Some need to play support roles, some need to be trained to interact compassionately with people in need, and some are already equipped by God to be on the front lines with the most desperate people.

4 LEARN FROM FAILURE.

Let's be honest: compassion ministries aren't as neat and clean—or as predictable—as many other ministries at the church. There will be a lot more loose ends and a lot more failures. If you can't live with failure by learning from it, you won't allow yourself to dive deeply into the needs of the community. If Steve Jobs, Elon Musk, and other entrepreneurs had been too cautious, they would never have invented the things that have revolutionized their industries. They failed repeatedly, but they learned persistently. Solomon used a farming metaphor to illustrate the necessity of the mess: "Where there are no oxen, the manger is empty, but from the strength of an ox come abundant harvests" (Proverbs 14:4).

GOD IS AT WORK BEHIND THE SCENES TO ACCOMPLISH HIS DIVINE PURPOSES WHETHER WE LABEL AN ACTIVITY A FAILURE OR A SUCCESS.

We have another factor at work in our lives: God is at work behind the scenes to accomplish His divine purposes whether we label an activity a failure or a success. It may be easy to see His hand in the obvious successes, but wise leaders learn to look for His hand even in the mistakes and bombs. In the parable of the sower, only one type of soil was productive. In this parable, if the seed of God's Word is sown and only 25 percent multiplies, what are we thinking when we expect perfection from all we do? It just doesn't make sense. We're throwing out seed all the time in all we do, so we can expect varied results, too.

⑤ BUILD A GREAT TEAM.

At first when we're starting an outreach ministry, we take anyone with a pulse to help us. As the ministry expands, we need to become more selective. For SERVE Days, we need a team that can do all the administrative tasks to set up the activities, collect the resources, provide the meals, secure photographers, and get stories to the pastor for the next morning's service. In Stage 2, churches that have a strong small-group ministry can connect groups with local organizations, and the synergy often works wonderfully well. Still, the person coordinating outreach needs a strong team to oversee and support these connections. In Stage 3, the expression of a sustained serve must have gifted staff (paid or not paid) and skilled volunteers to provide quality care and keep costs under control.

Of course, you want people who are passionate about the cause, but as the outreach ministry develops, you need passion combined with wisdom and administrative talents. The stresses of this ministry can be significant (even overwhelming), so make decisions about your team very carefully and slowly. You'll probably end up with a team composed of a few of the ten percenters who live to do outreach and a few who are more passionate about creating systems that work exceptionally well—and these people see outreach as a good place to use their administrative talents. Treasure them all, and forge them into a team that is excited and wise, compassionate and effective.

> **" TREASURE THEM ALL, AND FORGE THEM INTO A TEAM THAT IS EXCITED AND WISE, COMPASSIONATE AND EFFECTIVE. "**

Compassion fatigue is a very real threat for those of us who care about disadvantaged communities. It's easy to lose perspective and try to shoulder the burden alone . . . but that'll wreck your life, your family, and your ministry. Be aware of the signs, and build systems and habits that keep you vitally connected to God's limitless love, forgiveness, wisdom and power.

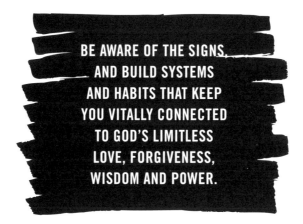

BE AWARE OF THE SIGNS, AND BUILD SYSTEMS AND HABITS THAT KEEP YOU VITALLY CONNECTED TO GOD'S LIMITLESS LOVE, FORGIVENESS, WISDOM AND POWER.

MICAH 6:7-8

Will the LORD be pleased with thousands of rams,
    with ten thousand rivers of olive oil?
Shall I offer my firstborn for my transgression,
    the fruit of my body for the sin of my soul?
He has shown you, O mortal, what is good.
    And what does the LORD require of you?
To act justly and to love mercy
    and to walk humbly with your God.

1

What are some signs that stress is starting to take a toll? What are some signs of full-blown burnout?

....

....

....

....

....

....

....

THINK ABOUT IT

2

Do you have at least one wise friend who is keeping you grounded and telling you some things about limits and boundaries, even if you don't want to hear it? If so, are you listening? If not, where can you find someone like this?

....

....

....

....

....

....

3

How would you describe
the talent and heart
of the people on your
outreach team? Do
you need to make any
adjustments? If so, what
are they?

....
....
....
....
....
....
....
....
....
....

4

Why is it important to
remember that God is at
work even in our failures
and even when we're not
active?

....
....
....
....
....
....
....
....
....
....

5

How would you help
someone suffering from
compassion fatigue?

....

....

....

....

....

....

....

....

....

....

....

....

....

....

....

....

....

....

....

....

Compassion is sometimes the fatal capacity for feeling what it is like to live inside somebody else's skin. It is the knowledge that there can never really be any peace and joy for me until there is peace and joy finally for you too.

FREDERICK BUECHNER
A Room Called Remember

CHAPTER EIGHT

SHAPING AND SHARPENING

AGAIN AND AGAIN

Again and again, we've seen that when disaster strikes, God's people jump in to help those in need. When Hurricane Matthew barreled through Haiti in late September of 2016, it was the first Category 5 storm in the Atlantic in almost a decade. By the time it reached the coast of South Carolina for its fourth landfall, it had weakened, but it still caused major damage. Manna Church has locations across the country and around the world, usually near military bases. When Matthew hit South Carolina, their church had people come out of the woodwork to help. Pastor Michael Fletcher and Outreach Pastor Dan Richardson, of Manna Church in Fayetteville, North Carolina, coordinated the volunteers they expected to show up . . . and the ones they'd never seen before. Many of these people had a military background, so they didn't need much training. They stepped up, got dirty, worked hard, and brought a blend of joy and determination to their care for people whose homes had been devastated by the winds and rain.

Michael and Dan already knew that people with a military background have extraordinary gifts, and they're never afraid of a big challenge. Their training has made them skilled and ready for disaster relief, but also, they're prepared to step into the most difficult and demanding tasks, like rescuing victims of human trafficking. Most churches need to take plenty of time to develop people with these skills, but soldiers, sailors, and airmen are ready to go. Manna Church also has a contingent of Navy Seals who attend. There's nothing those guys can't handle!

These two leaders instantly recognized the extraordinary talents already existing in the people in their church. But they're not alone. As we dive deeper into engaging our communities, we'll almost certainly find a deep well of resources that have been in our churches all along. As we identify these people, inspire them, and channel their efforts, we'll continually shape and sharpen our outreach ministry.

Sometimes, the next steps in this ministry are quite evident—we can't miss them. But it doesn't hurt to think through important elements of communicating clearly, building great leaders, and staying on track.

AS WE IDENTIFY THESE PEOPLE, INSPIRE THEM, AND CHANNEL THEIR EFFORTS, WE'LL CONTINUALLY SHAPE AND SHARPEN OUR OUTREACH MINISTRY.

★ EVALUATE YOUR MESSAGING.

The leader's passion is obvious to the people listening. If you're preaching a lot about prayer, your people will be praying. If end times eschatology finds its way into every sermon, your people will learn to see life primarily through that lens. If you talk a lot about generosity, your people will open their wallets. If you hemorrhage about the plight of the poor, the sick, the disabled, the overlooked, and the disadvantaged, your people will bleed for the brokenhearted.

Your culture should reinforce and accelerate your vision and mission. At Church of the Highlands, everything we do is designed to help people "know God, find freedom, discover purpose, and make a difference." Our weekend services help people experience the power, pardon, and presence of God. Our small groups help people apply the truth of God's Word so they find freedom. And our outreach teams tap into people's God-given purpose and give them opportunities to make a tangible, significant difference in the lives of others.

But we tend to drift. If we're not careful, our passion can wane, and all the trivia of administration can consume us. Then we focus far too much on what happens inside the church building instead of what happens outside. At one point, I realized we had been celebrating the efforts of childcare workers, ushers, and others who serve within the walls of the church. I then began also celebrating those who serve outside our walls. And I showed them pictures of how our people were making a difference in the lives of those in our community.

I realized I needed to make a series on compassion a regular part of the liturgical year. At Church of the Highlands, we devote the Sundays in July to "giving your life away" in all its forms, and during October and November, our messages are about generosity. So, fully one fourth of our calendar is given to sermons about compassion, and we pepper this emphasis in every other series throughout the year. That's who we are; that's our culture.

Never use guilt to motivate people to care for others. Point them to the wonder of God's grace toward them, share your own stories of involvement with needy people, and remind them that God has given them opportunities to step into the lives of others to make a difference—in many cases, a life-changing difference—if they'll recognize these moments and trust God to use them. Like Abraham, we're blessed to be a blessing. God wants to use us to change the direction of people's lives, and certainly, the destination of their eternity. Encourage your people to never underestimate the power of what God has done in their lives. They have a story to tell, and a world is waiting to listen.

In your motivation, don't focus primarily on the needs. Yes, you'll point out the very real needs, but talk more about what God is doing to meet those needs, and especially, how people sitting next to them in the service are actively involved in changing the trajectory of lives in the community. This dual picture of helplessness and hope, tragedy and triumph, gives your people a sense that God can use them to make a difference.

When we encourage all our people to come out to a SERVE Day, we know only half of them will show up, but we never shame the half that stayed home. On the next day in church, we celebrate how God has used our church to touch people and change lives. We don't say, "God used half our people"; we say, "God used you, the people of God," and we tell a lot of stories about what happened the previous day.

Outreach is never about guilt. It's living the gospel of grace. When God's amazing love takes root in a person's soul, they don't limit their engagement to SERVE Days. They notice needs all around them—in their neighborhood, at work, in school, at church, when they watch the news, as they read the paper, as they listen to friends, and everywhere they find out what's really going on in people's lives. Outreach is about acts of kindness, often random acts of kindness, and in the three stages, organized acts of kindness. Engaging the community is primarily about listening first before we take any steps of action. Only in listening can we discern the real needs below the obvious needs, and only in listening can we build trust. This is the kind of culture I believe God wants every church to create because it's central to the heart and mission of God.

A church's culture will always find expression: if you're not regularly talking about caring for broken people, it's not your culture . . . yet.

★ LEADERS LEAD.

From the beginning, I didn't tell people what they ought to do. I led by example, and I've got to tell you, it was fun! I led when we gave out bottled water, when we loaded up a truck with two pallets of rat bait and drove around town to offer it to people, when a truckload of bananas showed up, and every other outreach in our community. Our people quickly realized that caring for people isn't optional for me. Actually, I haven't had to think very much about changing a church culture because I'm one of those ten percenters who get up in the morning thinking about the needs of people. As I've taught and trained other pastors, though, I've seen the importance of reinforcing the principle that we have to lead from the front. People are watching us—people in the community, certainly, but also people in our churches.

OUTREACH IS NEVER ABOUT GUILT. IT'S LIVING THE GOSPEL OF GRACE.

★ MEASURE YOUR EFFORTS.

It's great to announce, "We're changing the world!" But soon, people want to know if you're actually touching very many lives. Here's the benchmark: Is the church growing? That's the primary indicator your outreach efforts are working.

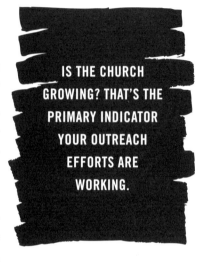

IS THE CHURCH GROWING? THAT'S THE PRIMARY INDICATOR YOUR OUTREACH EFFORTS ARE WORKING.

But there are other things to measure. It takes a little work, but it's important to have some quantitative measurements of a church's outreach. At the most basic level in Stage 1, we can measure the number of lawns we've mowed, the number of rooms we've cleaned, and the number of people who showed up to hear us sing at the nursing home. In Stage 2, we can measure how many addicts and alcoholics are in groups we sponsor, how many sacks of groceries we've given away, how many people have gone through our job training classes, the number of ex-cons who have been placed in homes and jobs, and how many single moms have been counseled and nurtured. Later, we can do a little more digging to find out how our Stage 3 sustained serve is affecting the community: if the crime rate has gone down, if there are fewer abandoned houses in the neighborhoods we serve, and if we see an increase in the number of families that have been reconciled. Of course, this list is just a taste of the enormous breadth of outreach activities we can measure. The point of measuring isn't to pat ourselves on the back, but to find out if we're using our resources most effectively for the kingdom of God. If not, what adjustments need to be made?

★ START WHERE YOU ARE AND WITH WHAT YOU HAVE.

In an outreach ministry, size isn't everything. All that matters is the heart of those who participate. Our first outreach at Healing Place Church was with 12 people passing out water, and our church's investment was $16. It was a rousing success!

If you have a church of 300 and 150 show up for an All Call SERVE Day, you've hit a home run. Then, after a year or so as some of your small groups develop partnerships and you have quarterly or monthly SERVE Days, you might have 30 people who regularly participate on those days. That's fantastic! Be encouraged, even if only a tenth of your people are devoted to compassion ministries. Celebrate them and showcase them on Sunday mornings. But still have at least one SERVE Day a year when everyone is encouraged to join in and you have very simple, family-friendly, effective activities.

★ CELEBRATE EVERY CONTRIBUTION.

If just ten percent of the people in a church live to care for those who desperately need help, how do we treat the other ninety percent? We celebrate them, too, for anything and everything they do to contribute to the life of the church—inside the walls and outside the walls. Some people are called to pray, some have the gift of generosity and give liberally to the causes of the church, some are musically gifted and serve on the worship team, and others are

IN AN OUTREACH MINISTRY, SIZE ISN'T EVERYTHING. ALL THAT MATTERS IS THE HEART OF THOSE WHO PARTICIPATE.

ushers who make people feel glad they walked through our doors. Everybody plays a part in the body, and we're thrilled with all of them.

Our task is to help all of our people connect their talents and contributions to God's heart for people outside the walls of the church. In the All Call, we invite everybody to participate in outreach, but we know only a small number of the people who show up that day are wired for consistent outreach efforts. Just as all of us are called to evangelize but only a few have the gift, all are called to be compassionate to those in need, but only a few have that unique gifting, calling and wiring. Those who don't aren't second-class Christians. In some way or another, everyone is contributing to the church's efforts to touch the lives of the poor.

★ WORK HARD TO MAKE THE FIRST STEP FUN, EASY, AND MEANINGFUL.

Your church's first All Call will be new to everybody, and every subsequent All Call will be a new experience for at least some people. These events are the entry point of service for the people in your church. Don't assume that because these activities are Stage 1 that you don't need to invest time in planning and preparation. If anything, they need more time and attention because for many people, SERVE Day is the first taste of active involvement in touching the lives for many people in your church.

> OUR TASK IS TO HELP ALL OF OUR PEOPLE CONNECT THEIR TALENTS AND CONTRIBUTIONS TO GOD'S HEART FOR PEOPLE OUTSIDE THE WALLS OF THE CHURCH.

By the time that day arrives, we've spent weeks and perhaps months identifying the very best

DON'T ASSUME THAT BECAUSE THESE ACTIVITIES ARE STAGE 1 THAT YOU DON'T NEED TO INVEST TIME IN PLANNING AND PREPARATION.

opportunities for SERVE Day, and we've gathered plenty of resources so people have what they need to fulfill their tasks. If anything, we make sure all our teams have more than enough tools, bags, and supplies to do what needs to be done. Many churches provide t-shirts for everyone for visual impact in the community. We usually start with a breakfast so everyone feels welcomed and nourished. This time also gives our leaders time to connect with each person on their teams to give clear directions about where they're going and what to expect when they get there. We launch the day with prayer. If we're all together at a breakfast, we pray before we leave. If we don't provide breakfast, we stream a pastor praying online so everybody feels connected and inspired as they go to their sites. If parents need to spend most (or all) of their SERVE Day corralling their kids, that's fine. It's all about creating a relaxed, fun, positive experience for everyone. We end the morning with a light lunch to bring everybody back together to celebrate how God used us. All of this requires careful planning and execution.

We have provided "outreach in a box" for individuals and families that came together to form a team on a SERVE Day, and these boxes also work for those who feel motivated when we don't have a scheduled SERVE Day. The box contains all they need: a clear explanation of the need and the goal for the day, the resources they'll need (or a list of resources they'll need to provide on their own), the location, and contact information if they have any questions.

★ REALIZE THE POWER OF STORIES.

A major part of the planning for outreach events is preparing to tell the stories at the celebration lunch and especially on Sunday. Have a skilled photographer or videographer on each site or traveling to all the sites to capture the work, but even more, the interaction between the people in your church and the people receiving help. Show faces, and share details that communicate heart, excitement, and impact. Of course, be discreet in sharing. Don't reveal anything that would embarrass the people you have served. (We usually ask for verbal permission of the adults whose pictures and stories we use, but we ask parents to sign a liability waiver for any pictures of children we use. Also, church staff members and specified photographers are the only ones allowed to take pictures of children—with, of course, a signed liability waiver.)

Statistics about hunger, human trafficking, addiction, and all the other needs are important, but they seldom move people's hearts like faces and stories. After every outreach, show the pictures and tell the stories of how God is using your people, and use social media to get the message out to far more people even more quickly. And pay attention to the conversations and posts people make about their experiences with the outreaches; join the conversation. This is often unvarnished and valuable feedback.

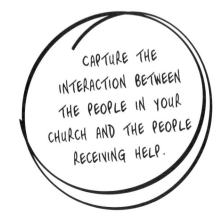

CAPTURE THE INTERACTION BETWEEN THE PEOPLE IN YOUR CHURCH AND THE PEOPLE RECEIVING HELP.

Create a landing spot for stories. Designate a person on your staff or a volunteer to capture the stories, edit them, and put them in forms that have the most impact in church services, in print, and online. We use forms we've created to get those who participate in SERVE Days to give us quick but vital information about their experience. Team leaders know this is an important part of the experience, so they're always looking for the best stories to share. They give suggestions to the people taking pictures and videos so they get heartwarming (and sometimes funny) stories from the day's events. They post messages and images on social media and use hashtags so they're easily accessible.

Manna Church in Fayetteville, North Carolina, provides "Acts of Kindness" cards in their lobby. They encourage their people to give the cards to people they've cared for, not just on SERVE Days but all day every day. The card invites the recipients to go online and share how the person's kindness has had an impact on them. In this way, the church hears stories from those who received acts of kindness, not only those who gave them.[1]

★ PREPARE FOR DISASTERS.

In Baton Rouge, we saw the devastation caused when Hurricane Katrina breached the levees in New Orleans and flooded much of the city. Our church sprang into action to care for the tens of thousands of displaced people. In Alabama, the coastal community sometimes is hit by hurricanes, but tornadoes are a real and present danger in much of the state. Wherever you live, it's wise for church leaders to have a contingency plan in place for natural disasters. They can identify skilled and available people, locate sources of resources, and craft a plan that can be implemented at

---

1   For more about Manna Church's outreach programs, go to https://capefear.mannachurch. org/outreach

a moment's notice. In some cases, such as hurricanes, we usually have at least a few days' warning. But others, like earthquakes and tornadoes, happen without a moment's notice. If we're ready, we can spring into action to be on the scene as soon as possible. [2]

★ ANTICIPATE RESPONSES.

As your church is involved in touching the lives of overlooked people in your community, a wide range of things will happen: A group of people in your church will find their true calling, and they'll be energized. People will be in touch with real needs, so they'll be more generous. A number of the people you serve will show up at church, and some will come to Christ and attend faithfully . . . and a few people won't like it. When those who don't look like us, talk like us, or smell like us show up, they make some people feel uncomfortable. Hopefully, our members will learn to open their hearts to those who are new, but a few may decide they'd rather go to a church were everybody is more like them . . . and that's okay.

In our second year in the church in Baton Rouge, we were reaching out to a pretty rough group of people. One Sunday when we invited people to come to the altar, I saw "the great divide": on one side were people who were well-dressed, groomed, all the appearances of having their life in order, and on the other side were those whose challenging lives were more apparent. They didn't know the "right" words, and they didn't know the "right" way to act, but they were responding to the invitation to give their lives to Jesus. Some of them were crying because the love of God was real to them for the first time. I thought it was one of the most beautiful moments I'd ever seen.

---

2   For much more on how we responded to disasters, look at Chapter 5 of *Servolution*.

After the service as people were leaving, a lady walked up to me. She spoke with great gravity: "Pastor, we have a problem."

I said, "Yes ma'am, tell me about it."

She looked at me and winced, "The sinners are outweighing the saints in this church." She paused for a second, and then told me, "Pastor, that's a problem with the anointing."

Instantly I tried to think of any passage of Scripture that would confirm her point of view, but I thought of all the scenes in the Gospels when outsiders and hurting people flocked to be near Jesus. I looked at this lady and told her, "I hope it will always be this way, and I don't think the Holy Spirit is displeased to have these people respond to Jesus."

I'm pretty sure she wasn't convinced. That was the last day she came to our church, but her granddaughter became a faithful member who gladly welcomed everyone who showed up at our door.

If you want to be a church that has a culture of serving both inside and outside the four walls, you need to visit Centerpoint Church in Chillicothe, Ohio. Pastors Chris and Kristyn VanBuskirk and their team have captured the essence of outreach, and a caring culture permeates the entire church. Sometimes we want to start "doing" outreach, but it may not be our identity yet. Caring for the community is woven into the identity of the team at Centerpoint.

> **WE ARE ALL ON THE GUEST SERVICES TEAM.**

"LOVING BROADLY ALWAYS RESULTS IN MAKING SOME PEOPLE FEEL UNCOMFORTABLE."

When a few of our ARC staff made a visit to Chillicothe, they were overwhelmed by the thoughtfulness and personal touch of this church family. From family BBQs to personalized gifts to Sunday team huddles, the culture values people. A team leader explained, "As greeters, we don't prop doors open with our butts. We open the door with our hands for every person that walks through." "We are all on the guest services team." And they live by that philosophy. Worship leaders, pastors, and the lead team are all engaged directly with welcoming people. We even saw the production manager, Rusty Penwell, leave the sound booth as church was just getting started to welcome first-time guests he had invited and help them find the nursery. That is the type of "preparing for response" we have to have. Where the "one" is actually our number one.

Loving broadly always results in making some people feel uncomfortable. Leaders are challenged to teach and model an inclusive love, but even if we do it perfectly, some people won't like it. It's a proven fact. Just ask Jesus.

★ REMAIN A LEARNER.

There will be problems. People will complain that we didn't do something right. Others will gripe that we left out some people who need our help. In any meaningful activity, criticism and pushback are inevitable. When it happens, respond with a ton of grace, listen carefully, thank people for their insights, and promise to do better next time.

I've organized outreaches that have been miserable failures. Remember: failure is always an option, but failing to care isn't. I'm not shocked when something doesn't work out, so I don't overreact and make the situation worse. That doesn't mean we settle for poor planning. Never. But in our planning, we always realize we're working with people who may have very little experience in compassion ministries, and we're caring for people with colossal problems. That mix usually produces incredible, wonderful results, but occasionally, it creates its own disaster. Learn from these misadventures. Stay calm and have a sense of humor. (How often do you think Jesus laughed when His team didn't understand their purpose or did dumb things?) Next time, things will go better. Next time, lives will be touched. Next time, someone will trust Christ and be rescued from hell. And next time is always just around the corner.

If we plan and coordinate ten outreaches on a SERVE Day and eight of them are hits but two don't work, that's a huge win for our church. Even on the two that weren't as successful, if the people on the team saw the leader respond with wisdom, patience, and good humor, it's still a big win for those people. They may not have ever seen a leader act like that, and it might inspire them to respond to their own problems with more faith, hope, and love. With good leaders, no situation is irredeemable.

> REMEMBER: FAILURE IS ALWAYS AN OPTION, BUT FAILING TO CARE ISN'T.

God often uses even the outreaches that bomb. We had a great idea to pass out chewing gum in the Target parking lot . . . until the security guard ran us off. The next day in church, a lady came to the altar to give her life to Christ. She explained that someone had given her a pack of gum

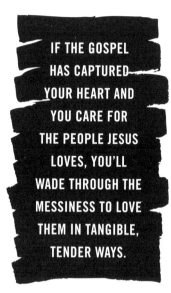

IF THE GOSPEL HAS CAPTURED YOUR HEART AND YOU CARE FOR THE PEOPLE JESUS LOVES, YOU'LL WADE THROUGH THE MESSINESS TO LOVE THEM IN TANGIBLE, TENDER WAYS.

and a card about the church the day before in a parking lot. We could have easily written off this outreach as a failure, but we were able to be present for enough time to reach this lady. And there may have been more seeds planted that we don't know about.

We rigorously evaluate our successes and our failures. Sometimes the idea was right but the timing or the leader wasn't right. Just because Mama burns the biscuits doesn't mean I don't go back into the kitchen. Outreach is messy, but it's not optional. It's central to the church's mission and culture. If you want an antiseptic, pristine church, don't be engaged in your community. But if the gospel has captured your heart and you care for the people Jesus loves, you'll wade through the messiness to love them in tangible, tender ways.

We also need to remember that not all outreaches are designed to have the same results. Some are planting, some are watering, and some are harvesting. In many of the activities on SERVE Days, we're engaging people in the community by just showing up to clean, sing, paint, hand out food, and care in a hundred other ways. With others, we're more actively involved in meeting specific needs, and with still others, we're deep in the weeds with people who struggle with seemingly unresolvable problems. And we never know how God might use us. One time we asked healthcare professionals to participate in a free medical clinic we were setting up for a day. A man who came that day got an exam, and the doctor discovered the man had prostate cancer. He was able to start getting treatment, and he even started coming to our church. He heard the gospel, and he came to Christ. In that experience, we saw all three phases of planting by offering free services, watering by pointing the man to treatment, and harvesting when he trusted in Jesus as his Savior.

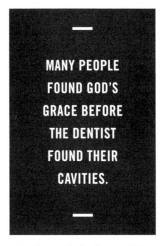

In a similar story, we created a mobile dental unit, donated by Joyce Meyer Ministries, offering free services. Before people sat in the chair, we gave them an opportunity to meet with a chaplain. Many people found God's grace before the dentist found their cavities.

It may sound strange, but we had a marriage outreach in which we offered to marry people for free. Yes, I know, some churches can't imagine performing marriages for people who aren't Christians, but we used these connections to show the love of God to people as they prepared to take one of the biggest steps of their lives, and many of them came to faith before their wedding or later when they came to our church.

We hosted a prom associated with our Birmingham Dream Center. At the event, we celebrated like crazy: we pampered the girls, provided them with prom dresses, got suits for the guys, set up a chocolate fountain and a photo booth, and in general, gave them a fantastic time! For many, it was the first and only prom they ever attended. Through the impact of that night, many have started to view themselves as valuable, have grown in their faith, and have joined our church community. Hundreds of churches around the world have participated with Tim Tebow's Night to Shine where people with special needs feel loved and treasured. Inevitably, at all events like this, at least a few people come to faith and find a church home. When we hosted the Easter Egg Hunt for kids with special needs, we were able to start a small group for these dear parents. We let the parents know our church is equipped to host them with wheelchair ramps and other accommodations—these simple things encouraged them to join our church family.

With a little creativity, the opportunities to touch people in our towns and cities is endless. Yes, sometimes we'll fall flat on our faces, but if we learn from each encounter, we'll be more effective for God's kingdom next time.

THE STORY CONTINUES

Caring for people in need isn't secondary to Jesus. The kingdom of God is the gospel of grace transforming us from the inside out so we love like Jesus loves (1 John 4:10–11), we forgive like Jesus forgives (Ephesians 4:32), and we accept people who are different from us the way Jesus accepts you and me (Romans 15:7).

The story of compassion never ends, and it's communicated the same way I told our class about my GI Joe—it's show and tell. Tangible expressions of love have a far greater impact than mere words. I came to faith because someone stopped to connect with me and demonstrate the love of God, and now I lead a ministry for people who are often overlooked. The woman who anointed Jesus' feet with perfume will never be forgotten, Jesus explained, because her love for Him was a response to His wonderful love for her. Jesus gravitated to people in need: crippled, lame, blind, sick, demon-possessed, hungry, confused, and ignored by society. His calling to us is to share His heart and follow His example to notice the people around us and let His love flow through us to them. Jesus used a ministry model of "show and tell" to move us to follow Him, and that's the model we use in outreach ministries.

By the power of the Holy Spirit, the people in our churches need to know the love of God more intimately, and they need us to help them connect their love with the people who are waiting to be touched by their generosity and care. And as people receive our help, God will work in them so they become channels of love to even more people. That's how the grace of God multiplies from one person to another and one generation to another: in words, yes, but also in compassionate action to meet real needs.

Those who have been overwhelmed with the incredible love of God have tender hearts and fierce determination to help those in need. Mother Teresa famously explained, "Love has a hem to her garment that reaches to the very dust. It sweeps the stains from the streets and lanes, and because it can, it must."

MARK 12:28-31

One of the teachers of the law came and heard them debating. Noticing that Jesus had given them a good answer, he asked him, "Of all the commandments, which is the most important?"

"The most important one," answered Jesus, "is this: 'Hear, O Israel: The Lord our God, the Lord is one. Love the Lord your God with all your heart and with all your soul and with all your mind and with all your strength.' The second is this: 'Love your neighbor as yourself.' There is no commandment greater than these."

1

What are some ways you can capture and use stories more effectively? What is the "landing spot" for stories generated by your church's activities?

....

....

....

....

....

....

....

2

What disasters have occurred in your area in the past decade or so? Was your church prepared to help those who were affected? What would a disaster relief plan look like for you and your church?

....

....

....

....

....

....

....

THINK ABOUT IT

3

For the people who have outreach ideas for the church, how will you respond to them and empower them?

....

....

....

....

....

....

....

....

....

....

4

Do you have a process they can follow that can make their idea a reality? How might small groups play a key role in making it happen?

....

....

....

....

....

....

....

....

....

....

5

Which of the stories in this book (or your own experiences of serving your community) inspired you the most? What about it (or them) is most meaningful?

....
....
....
....
....
....
....
....
....
....

6

What's the next step in shaping and sharpening your church's outreach ministry to your community?

....
....
....
....
....
....
....
....
....
....

ACKNOWLEDGEMENTS

DeLynn

I could do nothing without your support, leadership, guidance, wisdom, and love. Thank you for your sacrifice through this project and life. Whatever good is in me I attribute to God and to you.

McCall, Dylan, and Isabella

The greatest gift God could ever give a man is those who bear his name. I'm so proud of how you live out your own show and tell for Jesus.

Vicki and Dan Ohlerking

DeLynn and I are so blessed as a couple to have you guys as friends for over 30 years. You've supported and believed in us, and nothing we've ever done could have happened without your contribution. Let's do another 30 years together!

Tori Townley, Ron Hogland, and Robert Record

Thanks to each of you for living out show and tell every day and for contributing so much to this message.

STEVE AND SUSAN BLOUNT, AND PAT SPRINGLE

From the very beginning of these ideas (and beyond), you guys have championed and crafted these words and passions. Thanks for being the best.

GABI FERRARA AND DAVID SONG (DESIGN TEAM)

You guys make everything easy. Your tireless effort and creativity have always been a source of help to everything we've done. Thank you.

JIMMY AND IRENE ROLLINS

Thanks for all the conversations and all the steering and directing for me to have a bigger heart of compassion, love, and show and tell. You guys live it every day.

KYLE AND LIZ TURNER

Thanks for your contribution and creative input on this project. Your wisdom and unique perspective on reaching people was so valuable to me.

GREG SURRATT, THE ARC TEAM, AND ARC CHURCHES

Thanks for what we get to do together: planting churches, helping pastors, and transforming communities with the love of Jesus. What Bro. Billy brought together continues to do God's work!

CHRIS HODGES AND THE CHURCH OF THE HIGHLANDS TEAM

I've never found a better friend, pastor, and leader than you, Pastor Chris. Thank you. You and the Highlands team live out show and tell for Jesus in a million ways. You guys are my heroes.

DREAMCENTER NETWORK

Thank you for being such a collective voice in so many diverse ways for the poor and hurting. Your tireless effort is inspiring.

PASTOR MATTHEW AND PASTOR TOMMY BARNETT

You guys are a constant model of the love of God for humanity. No one has ever inspired me like you guys have.

...AND THERE ARE SOME FRIENDS I JUST WOULDN'T WANT TO DO LIFE WITHOUT:

MC Lee

Lee Burns

Whittle

Mawae #68

Jope

Jeffery

Siebeling

Stovall

Mayo

Steve R

Ketterling

MC

D Neece

MWS

Ray[2]

Cool Daddy and Kim

Klein

ABOUT THE AUTHOR

Thirty-five years of ministry experience, including 20 years planting and pastoring a megachurch and several years leading a national church-planting network, brings considerable opportunity to share with others what you've learned about living, loving and leading. For Dino Rizzo, these years of ministry have allowed him to pursue his passions for his Savior, his family and the church.

Five years after marrying, Dino and DeLynn, 28 and 23 at the time, started Healing Place Church in Baton Rouge with a single focus of being a "healing place for a hurting world." From the beginning, the Rizzos wanted to help people.

In 2000, Dino co-founded the Association of Related Churches (ARC), a growing group of churches devoted to launching, connecting, and equipping churches and pastors—with the ultimate vision of seeing a life-giving church in every community in the world. Dino serves as the Executive Director for ARC, which has launched hundreds of local churches and is poised to train, equip, and resource hundreds of other couples as they plant churches in the coming years.

In his ARC role, Dino leads the National Serve Day initiative, enlisting ARC churches to serve their communities on a specific, designated day—hoping and praying that serving will become part of every church's DNA.

Dino also serves on the Executive Team and is Outreach and Missions Pastor for Church of the Highlands in Birmingham, Alabama, one of the largest and most influential churches in the United States, led by church planter and Senior Pastor Chris Hodges. In these roles, Dino teaches in weekend worship services throughout the year and leads the church to serve the community.

For years, Dino has talked and walked out God's call to His people to serve others. In 2009, he released the best-selling book Servolution: Starting a Church Revolution Through Serving. The book's success launched a movement of more than 700 churches throughout the world that participate in Servolution in their communities, including Lakewood Church (Houston, Texas), Lifechurch.tv, Camina De Vida (Lima, Peru), Life Church (Manurew, New Zealand) and Assembly of God (Gdansk, Poland). With Servolution, Dino sounded a call to churches that serving is not about an event, but rather, about infusing a "serving culture" into their DNA. Dino continues to hear from leaders who tell him about the transformational impact that Servolution has made in their church and city.

Dino and DeLynn have three children, McCall, Dylan and Isabella, and they are a testimony to all that God has done through their lives.

DON'T DO MINISTRY ALONE.

It's not just about the mission, it's about the relationship we have with God and with each other. Whether you are looking to launch, connect or equip your church, ARC is for you.

WE ARE AN ASSOCIATION OF RELATIONAL CHURCHES WORKING WITH CHURCH PLANTERS AND CHURCH LEADERS TO PROVIDE SUPPORT, GUIDANCE, AND RESOURCES TO LAUNCH AND GROW LIFE-GIVING CHURCHES.

WE LAUNCH

We have a highly successful, proven model for planting churches with a big launch day to gain the initial momentum needed to plant a church. We train church planters, and we provide a tremendous boost in resources needed.

WE CONNECT

We provide dozens of opportunities to connect with other church planters, veteran pastors, leadership mentors, as well as friends who are walking the same path as you are. You're never short on opportunities to connect!

WE EQUIP

Our team continually creates and collects great ministry resources that will help you and your church be the best you can be. As part of this family, you get to draw water from a deep well of experience in ministry.

LAUNCHING, CONNECTING, & EQUIPPING THE LOCAL CHURCH

ARCCHURCHES.COM   @ARCCHURCHES   /WEPLANTLIFE

ADDITIONAL RESOURCES

TO ORDER COPIES OF *SERVE YOUR CITY*, *SERVE YOUR CITY SMALL GROUP LEADER'S GUIDE AND PARTICIPANT'S GUIDE*, AND *SERVOLUTION*, GO TO ARCCHURCHES.COM

STAGE 1 RESOURCES

Go to **serveday.today** to find:

- Outreach Ideas and How To Manuals (English and Spanish)
  - Free Car Prep
  - Backpack Buddies Ministry
  - Laundry Mat Outreach
  - Rooms of Refuge Ministry
  - More available online
- SERVEday planning docs (includes prayer focuses, timelines, budgeting, outreach ideas, and more)
- Christmas Shopping Mall Planning Docs
- LOVE WEEK Planning Doc

DOWNLOADABLE PROMO GRAPHICS

Examples:

- SERVEday Promo Graphics (Email headers, IG profiles, banners, etc.)
- SERVE Shirt design
- Outreach Card Design

ONLINE TRAININGS AND TEACHINGS

Examples:

- SERVEbrews and webinars
- Online Video Resources
- Access to closed FB group conversation when your church registers for SERVEday

STAGE 2 AND 3 RESOURCES

Go to **servolution.org** to find resources such as:

- Adopt a Block Manual
- Mobile Dream Center manual

Join the DC Network at **www.dreamcenter.org/dc-network** for access to things like downloadable resources, name copyright, and video calls.

**FOR MORE FROM PASTOR DINO
VISIT DINORIZZO.COM**